WRITERS AND CRITICS

Chief Editor
A. NORMAN JEFFARES

Advisory Editors
DAVID DAICHES
C. P. SNOW

Sean O'Casey is unquestionably one of the greatest dramatists of our century: his reputation, in spite of the misgivings of some critics about his later plays, as secure as that of Shaw and Synge. The author in this study provides relevant information about O'Casey's life and times to explain the dramatist's unique achievement, and then goes on to a critical evaluation of the plays. All the major works (a chapter has also been devoted to the autobiographies) are discussed in detail, and the most significant pieces of criticism pertaining to them embodied in the study. Most of O'Casey's minor works are referred to, and the excellence in them highlighted. A select bibliography is included: not only of books and articles referred to in this study but also those likely to throw light on the man and his works.

Saros Cowasjee is an Assistant Professor at the University of Saskatchewan, Regina, Canada, where he specialises in Irish drama. A graduate of the Universities of Agra and Leeds, he is the author of *Sean O'Casey: the Man Behind the Plays* (Oliver & Boyd, 1963, St. Martin's Press, 1964; Oliver & Boyd, revised paperback edition, 1965).

O'CASEY

SAROS COWASJEE

OLIVER AND BOYD
EDINBURGH AND LONDON

OLIVER AND BOYD LTD
Tweeddale Court
Edinburgh 1

39A Welbeck Street
London W. 1

~~1920~~
~~1956~~
~~015~~

First published 1966

PRINTED IN GREAT BRITAIN BY
OLIVER AND BOYD LTD., EDINBURGH

CONTENTS

ACKNOWLEDGMENTS

For permission to quote from O'Casey's works acknowledgments are due to Macmillan & Co. Ltd, the Macmillan Company of Canada Ltd and St Martin's Press Inc. (*Juno and the Paycock, The Shadow of a Gunman, The Plough and the Stars, The Silver Tassie*); to Macmillan & Co. Ltd, the Macmillan Company of Canada Ltd and the Macmillan Company, New York (*Within the Gates, The Star Turns Red, Purple Dust, Red Roses for Me, I Knock at the Door, Pictures in the Hallway, Drums under the Window, Inishfallen Fare Thee Well, Rose and Crown*); to Macmillan & Co. Ltd and University of Missouri Press (*Feathers from the Green Crow*); and to W. H. Allen & Co. and George Braziller Inc. (*The Green Crow*).

For permission to quote from the works of other authors acknowledgments are also due to the Macmillan Company, New York, and MacGibbon & Kee Ltd (David Krause, *Sean O'Casey, The Man and His Work*); and to St Martin's Press Inc. (Robert Hogan, *The Experiments of Sean O'Casey*).

The photograph on the front cover is reproduced by permission of Radio Times Hulton Picture Library.

ABBREVIATED TITLES
BY WHICH O'CASEY'S WORKS
AND OTHERS ARE CITED

O'CASEY'S WORKS

References are to *Collected Plays* for all plays
included in its four volumes

C.P.	=	*Collected Plays.*
D.U.W.	=	*Drums Under the Window.*
F.G.C.	=	*Feathers from the Green Crow.*
G.C.	=	*The Green Crow.*
I.F.T.W.	=	*Inishfallen Fare Thee Well.*
I.K.D.	=	*I Knock at the Door.*
J.P.	=	*Juno and the Paycock.*
P.H.	=	*Pictures in the Hallway.*
P.S.	=	*The Plough and the Stars.*
S.G.	=	*The Shadow of a Gunman.*
S.T.	=	*The Silver Tassie.*
W.G.	=	*Within the Gates.*

OTHERS

Cowasjee	=	SAROS COWASJEE: *Sean O'Casey: the Man Behind the Plays.*
Hogan	=	ROBERT HOGAN: *The Experiments of Sean O'Casey.*
Krause	=	DAVID KRAUSE: *Sean O'Casey, the Man and his Work.*

CHAPTER I

THE FORMATIVE YEARS

Nowhere in Europe were living conditions more loathsome than in the Dublin of O'Casey's youth. In old and dilapidated Georgian houses, originally designed to hold a single family, the poor were crowded in incredible numbers: living a life of misery, squalor, and filth inconceivable to those who have not experienced them. O'Casey, who faced the full blast of the evils of tenement life, recalled a tenement scene years later:

> Then, where we lived, with thousands of others, the garbage of the ashpit with the filth from the jakes was tumbled into big wicker baskets that were carried on the backs of men whose clothing had been soaked in the filth from a hundred homes; carried out from the tiny back yards, through the kitchen living-room, out by the hall, dumped in a horrid heap on the street outside, and left there, streaming [*sic*] out stench and venom, for a day, for two days, maybe for three, till open carts, sodden as the men who led the sodden horses, came to take the steaming mass away, leaving an odour in the narrow street that lingered till the wind and the rain carried trace and memory far into outer space or into the heaving sea.[1]

The inquiry commissioned by the British Government into Dublin housing conditions in November 1913 revealed some astonishing facts. There were in the city 5,322 tenement houses accommodating 25,822 families—almost one-third of the city's total population. Of these, 20,108 families occupied one room each, in which they performed all the functions of life and death. In 1924, the year *Juno and the Paycock* was first performed, there were 40,000 families inhabiting single rooms in extreme poverty and wretchedness. The mortality rate in 1880, the year of O'Casey's birth, was 44·8 per thousand; twenty years later it rose to 46 per thousand: well over twice as high as in English cities of the same population. Two Commissions of Inquiry squarely blamed this high death rate on the evils of tenement life. Papers and journals highlighted the tragic figures and denounced the living conditions in the strongest of words, but nothing substantial seemed to come of it.

It is necessary to keep this gruesome picture of Dublin before us. It is this Dublin that shaped O'Casey and made of him the dramatist that he came to be; it alone explains his strength and his weakness and gives a clue to the many contradictions and enigmas that surround him. The seeds of his idealism, pacifism, communism, and all his other "-isms" were sown in tenement houses and watered with grinding poverty. Though later he was to leave the grim conditions of his younger days far behind him, he refused to dissociate himself from his past. Replying to critics who tried to dismiss him as "a slum dramatist" and "a gutter-snipe who could jingle a few words together," O'Casey wrote:

> The terms were suitable and accurate for he was both, and, all his life, he would hold the wisdom and courage that these conditions had given him. Wheresoever he would go, whomsoever he might meet, be the places never so grandiloquent and rich, the persons never so noble in rank and origin, he, O'Casey, would ever preserve, ever wear—though he would never flaunt it—the tattered badge of his tribe.[2]

Few men have worn a badge better; fewer still have remained so loyal to bygone days and causes.

Sean O'Casey was born in Dublin on 31 Mar. 1880.

Named John, which he later Gaelicised to Sean, he was the last of several children, of whom only three brothers and a sister were to grow beyond childhood. His father, Michael O'Casey, was the son of a mixed marriage between a Catholic man and a Protestant woman. Brought up in the faith of his mother, he had endless trouble with his Catholic brothers and sisters. So one day, "without as much as a goodbye or a kiss me arse,"[3] he left his people and came to Dublin, where he married Susan Archer. A brave, honest, and learned man, he worked hard to earn his two pounds a week to keep the family together. But a spinal injury finished him off when Johnny was still a child.

The death of Michael O'Casey brought more than poverty and hardship—it led to the disintegration of the family. Johnny's two elder brothers, Michael and Tom, joined the Army; his sister Ella married a bugler, one Nicholas Benson. Johnny, with his mother and his third brother Archie, moved into a cheaper house. Here the three lived on the fifteen shillings a week that Archie sweated for in the publishing house of the *Daily Express*, and slept between the puff felts he skilfully pilfered from his employers. Most of the meals consisted of dry bread and tea; a bit of meat or fish, whenever it could be had, turned this into a feast. Johnny's clothes were in rags; his shoes were re-inforced with cardboard soles, which soaked up the water and made him pray as he hastened to attend the Sunday school: "Oh God, give me a new pair of boots, a new pair of boots."[4]

Deprived of a father, ignored by his brothers and sister, Johnny had no one in the world save his mother to look after him. She nursed his ulcerated eyes, took him regularly to an ophthalmic hospital for treatment, and stood between him and every harm. Even though she was devoutly religious, she defied her parish priest who wanted Johnny to present himself at the school for a sound thrashing. In return, O'Casey more than repaid her by his tender care of her in her old age. He stayed by her side till her death, and then went on to immortalise her in play after play. The spirit of Susan flames in all the early O'Casey heroines: "in the brave but rash Minnie Powell in *The Shadow of a Gunman*, in the nagging but heroic Juno in *Juno and the Paycock*, in the weak but affectionate Nora Clitheroe in *The Plough and the Stars*."[5] Even in the much later play, *Red Roses for Me* (1943), the character of Mrs Breydon is clearly based on his mother's and through Ayamonn (modelled on the young Sean O'Casey) he thanks her for all that she had done for him: "It's I who know that well: when it was dark, you always carried the sun in your hand for me; when you suffered me to starve rather than thrive towards death in an Institution, you gave me life to play with as a richer child is given a coloured ball."[6]

Because of the pain in his eyes and the need to attend the hospital regularly, Johnny's schooling began rather late. It ended soon and abruptly, when he brought the heavy ebony ruler down "on the pink, baldy, hoary oul' head of hoary oul' Slogan"[7]—the schoolmaster who had caned him unjustly and mercilessly. Out in the world, unlettered, he joined the ranks of unskilled workers. Errand-boy, dispatch clerk, dockworker, hod-carrier, stone-breaker, and janitor were some of the jobs he was to hold before he could risk living by writing alone. Between one job and another there were long intervals of unemployment, when he suffered extreme poverty and hunger. Years later, when he was a successful Abbey dramatist and could add a slice of bacon and potatoes to his accustomed diet of dry bread and tea, he told his friend Gabriel Fallon: "Never use the word 'hunger' . . . until you have gone without food for three whole days. Otherwise, you don't know its meaning."[8] O'Casey knew what hunger meant and the best scenes in his plays and the best passages in his autobiographies bear witness to this. O'Casey cannot portray the rich and the

well-fed: all his immortal characters come straight from
the slums.

Denied formal schooling, Johnny began to educate
himself. When he was about fourteen years old he could
read, skipping the biggest words, the stories in *The Boys
of London and New York* and in the various penny adventure
books. Later, he plunged into books left by his father:
Merle d'Aubigné's *History of the Reformation*, Sullivan's
Geography Generalised, and an American book called *The
Comprehensive Summary*. He read widely but unsystematic-
ally, revelling in the works of Byron, Shelley, Keats,
Goldsmith, Crabbe, and Tennyson. From his meagre
salary he saved pennies to buy himself books: Dickens,
because he was cheap, *Chambers's Dictionary*, because it
was absolutely essential. One day be bought the Globe
edition of Shakespeare for a shilling and found himself
on the threshold of a new life. Later on, the writings of
Frazer, Darwin, Ruskin, and Shaw were to influence
his thinking profoundly and to weaken his faith in
religion. He read the Bible, too, and by the time he
came to write his plays he knew much of it by heart.

At that time, Dublin was seething with political and
social unrest, and O'Casey was drawn into the activities
of the various political organisations. The first to win
his allegiance was the Gaelic League, which he joined
in 1903. Though primarily a language movement
founded by Dr Douglas Hyde in 1893, it had achieved
a political status. Sean was so enthusiastic for the Gaelic
cause that every evening, when he laid aside his shovel,
he would rush to one of the League schools to sweep the
floors, to learn Gaelic, and to teach it to others. Among
the League members were the supporters of the Irish
Republican Brotherhood, lineal descendant of the
Fenian Organisation, and they induced Sean to join
them. Sean was now devoting much of his time and
energy to the I.R.B.; he was intently absorbed in a
movement that promised his country freedom. He soon

found, however, that the members were much too
romantically inclined to be really effective:

> They were immersed in the sweet illusion of fluttering
> banners, of natty uniforms, bugle-blow marches,
> with row on row of dead and dying foemen strewn over
> the Macgillicuddy's Reeks, the Hills of Dublin, and
> the bonny blue Mountains of Mourne, with the
> *Soldier's Song* aroaring at the dawning of the day. All
> guns and drums, but no wounds. Not a thought,
> seemingly, about the toil, the rotten sweat, the craving
> for sleep, the sagging belly asking silently for food;
> the face disfigured, one eye wondering where the
> other had gone; an arm twisted into a circle or a figure
> of eight; the surprised lung, bullet-holed, gasping for
> breath; or the dangling leg, never to feel firm on the
> earth again.[9]

Moreover, it was becoming increasingly clear to him
that the first battle in Ireland should be fought against
Irish poverty, not for Irish freedom: "the real struggle
was not between the English Imperialist and the Irish
Republican, but between international capitalism and
the workers of the world."[10] His attempt to get the
I.R.B. to support Labour and his sharp criticism of
Republican policy made him unpopular. He gradually
dissociated himself from the I.R.B. to join the Labour
leader Jim Larkin and help organise the Irish Transport
and General Workers' Union. Still he remained committed to Republican ideals and helped the Republicans
in every way he could. He wrote vigorously in *The Irish
Worker* to make the Republicans see that their strength
lay in recruiting the thousands of hungry workers to
their ranks. The Rising of 1916, however, completed
his disillusionment with revolutionary Republicanism.
The Plough and the Stars is a vivid dramatisation of this
disillusionment.

Sean had an unqualified admiration for Larkin and

the zeal with which he worked to organise the labourers in Dublin. At the time of the Great Dublin Lockout of 1913, which was caused by the workers' refusal to pledge themselves against Larkin's Union, O'Casey lost the job that had kept him and his mother alive. Himself unhappy, he strove to make life bearable for the workers who had lost their jobs. He organised entertainments and social evenings for them at Liberty Hall. Later, when the workers formed the Irish Citizen Army, Sean became its first secretary. He found it difficult to get along with Captain J. R. White, the Chairman of the Army Council, and Countess Markievicz, the treasurer, and after an abortive attempt to dislodge the Countess, he resigned.

On Easter Monday, 24 Apr. 1916, the Irish Citizen Army with the Irish Volunteers struck a blow for Irish liberty. Ironically, O'Casey, whose whole life had been dedicated to Ireland's struggle, took no part; he was imprisoned for the night in a church and then detained in a granary. It is just as well it happened that way, for how else could we have had *The Plough and the Stars*? Enough has been said of the men who fought in Easter Week; O'Casey tells us something about those men who did not fight and thereby decided the fate of the Rising.

Robert Hogan is right in asserting that "for O'Casey the Great Lockout was the crucial public event of his first forty years . . . that it solidified in him the yet unaltered conviction that a man of good will must strive for the international abolition of poverty and the ownership of the means of production by the worker."[11] But the rising had an equally profound influence on him: it completed his disillusionment with the use of revolutionary means to gain political ends. Later, when the Civil War divided Irishmen into factions, and led them to atrocities before which British outrages against the Irish seem pale, O'Casey remained completely aloof. He who had suffered hunger and privation knew what man's first need was. He joined the tiny Socialist Party of Ireland and went about campaigning for food for hungry children. The Rising marked the end of a phase in O'Casey's thinking.

Until recently, we knew very little about Sean O'Casey's early writings. O'Casey makes sketchy allusions in his autobiographies to things he wrote in his twenties and thirties, but these lay largely buried in dust-coated library files unknown even to students writing dissertations on his works. What some scholars did succeed in getting hold of were pamphlets such as *Song of the Wren* (1918), *The Sacrifice of Thomas Ashe* (1918), and *The Story of the Irish Citizen Army* (1919). Occasionally an article or two published in some Dublin paper, which had long since wound up, would come their way. And on the strength of this little they would try to show the birth and growth of a dramatist. The result, of course, was not altogether satisfactory: Jules Koslow in *The Green and the Red* (1949) and Robert Hogan in *The Experiments of Sean O'Casey* (1960) wisely steer clear of O'Casey's apprentice writings, while David Krause in *Sean O'Casey: the Man and His Work* (1960) and I in my *Sean O'Casey: the Man Behind the Plays* (1963) tried hard to draw conclusions from insufficient material.

Robert Hogan has now given us a fine selection of O'Casey's writings between 1905 and 1925, under the title *Feathers from the Green Crow* (1962). Though I do not agree with some of Hogan's opinions, I admire the skill with which he has assembled the material into related groups and have much respect for his editorial comments. In his introduction to the book, Hogan says:

This selection from old newspapers, magazines, pamphlets, and manuscripts is a testament to struggle and to courage, for every bit of it was composed under conditions which most writers would find impossible—not to write in, but to survive in. . . .[12]

In a sense, this book may be taken as documentation for an autobiography. The opinions in the stories and songs and essays were all O'Casey's; some of them he would disagree with today, for this period was one of growth. The opinions in the connecting notes are all mine; if I have misread his growth, the work is there to correct me.

I have wondered if I am doing the playwright a disservice by resurrecting some of this material. This problem I have pondered for some months, because I would wittingly do no disservice to a man whose work I have as strongly admired as I have ineptly discussed.[13]

There can be no question that much of the writing included in this volume was written under very difficult conditions. It is also true that this selection is a documentation for an autobiography; more, perhaps an autobiography in its own right. It is equally true that no disservice has been done to Sean O'Casey by making these writings available to the public, though much of the material is downright poor. Hogan, I feel, knows this and pleads in vain when he writes: "Unlike Joyce, O'Casey did not consider himself dedicated to literature; and most of this early work was written for some immediate, nonliterary purpose,"[14] and "He was not greatly interested in beauty of expression, even though he sometimes grew intoxicated with words."[15] That O'Casey was dedicated to literature, at least to literature in its broadest sense, is borne out in his autobiographies; that he was striving for "beauty of expression" can be seen in the futile attempts he makes at style. He quotes from his favourite authors freely, and plagiarises even more freely. Almost every one of his early newspaper articles is prefaced with a quotation, which often has little relevance to the subject under discussion.

There is not much to be said for O'Casey's songs,

published under the titles *Songs of the Wren* and *More Wren Songs* by Fergus O'Connor in 1918. These were written over several years, and the author was paid £5 for the full copyright by the publishers. A selection from the two "Wren" pamphlets is included in *Feathers from the Green Crow*. The most popular of them, and the author's favourite, was "The Grand Oul' Dame Britannia," which Lady Gregory included in her *Kiltartan History Book* in 1926. A few of these songs show the influence of Byron and Burns; the former's influence is most perceptible in "Mary is Faithful to Me." Most of the other songs are satiric comments on the First World War and Britain's attempt to recruit the Irish to fight for her.

In 1918 there also appeared *The Sacrifice of Thomas Ashe*, which was an improved version of an earlier lament called *The Story of Thomas Ashe*. Here O'Casey recalls the last days of Ashe, an Irish patriot and a member of the Citizen Army, who died as a result of forcible feeding in Dublin's Mountjoy Prison. The following year saw the publication of *The Story of the Irish Citizen Army*—a failure both as history and literature. It was an occasion for O'Casey to air his views on the Rising and the various movements and personalities connected with it. One critic, writing under the initials "E.O'D." [Eimar O'Duffy] in *The Irish Statesman* of 12 Jul. 1919, scathingly but accurately remarked: "The actions and attitudes of the national movement are judged, or misjudged, entirely in reference to their bearing on the labouring section of the nation; and the worth of each and every prominent Nationalist is estimated from his attitude towards the social and economic views held by Mr O'Cathasaigh [O'Casey's Gaelicised name]." It is no surprise that O'Casey judged James Connolly, the leader of the Irish Citizen Army, rather severely, for though a Labour man Connolly was shifting his loyalties to the Irish Volunteers—from Labour to Nationalism.

The core of the book is a paean in praise of Jim Larkin.

Mr Hogan has done no disservice to O'Casey by making these early writings available to the public, and I have done no disservice to O'Casey by dismissing them as slight works. O'Casey's reputation has passed the stage when it could be seriously affected by critics and their criticism; moreover, to see merit where no merit is visible is to do the author a singular disservice. However, this volume contains bits and pieces good enough to be placed beside O'Casey's later satirical writings. Hogan has made no mention of these in his editorial comments, and no reviewer to my knowledge has referred to them either. Here is O'Casey attacking a corrupt railway official in "Chiefs of the G.N.R.I., III," published in *The Irish Worker* of 15 Feb. 1913:

Henry, Hugh, or Herbert Milling was a remarkable man. He was originally an Englishman, and, as is well known, a prophet is never honoured in his own country, he shook its dust from his feet one day, embarked on a ship, came over to the "Emerald Isle," was received with open arms by the officials of the G.N.R., who fell on his neck and kissed him. He has been here ever since. He bears on his lofty brow the sure mark of election. Anxiety and wistfulness for the company's success have furnished him with a grey head, trembling hand, and haggard cheek. No one who knew him well would venture to doubt that the Company's interests were only to be considered second to his own. . . .

H. Milling, Esq., was a young "sport." He, like most people, knew how to enjoy himself; but, unlike many, he found many opportunities. I often wondered when I saw him in his natty, nautical costume of reefer jackets, blue pants and peaked hat, was he on a holiday, who gave him that holiday, or was he enjoying himself on the Company's time? Well, of course, Mr. Milling could not walk on the sea, so he built himself a yacht. When was the yacht built? Well, it wasn't a work carried out so publicly as the building of the Ark by Noah. It was put together by the Company's men in the "Test Room" at the Permanent Way Stores, Dublin, and I'm told many amusing scenes occurred of "clapping to the door" when anybody particular was knocking around. Everyone, of course, heard the story that the men were paid by Milling himself, but even so, what bye-law, rule, or regulation of the Company permits its men being utilised in this way for the pleasure of officials who are woefully overpaid already?[16]

The sarcasm and irony shoots out of the simple straight-forward sentences and Mr Herbert Milling is completely demolished. O'Casey is at his best when he is original, when he writes what he feels and not what he has learnt. For instance, the best lines in *Juno and the Paycock* are not, decidedly not, the oft-quoted prayer of Mrs Tancred—

Mother o' God, Mother o' God, have pity on the pair of us! . . . O Blessed Virgin, where were you when me darlin' son was riddled with bullets, when me darlin' son was riddled with bullets! . . . Sacred Heart of the Crucified Jesus, take away our hearts o' stone . . . an' give us hearts o' flesh! . . . Take away this murdherin' hate . . . an' give us Thine own eternal love!—[17]

which is obviously adapted from Shelley's *Adonais* and Ezekiel XI. 19. The best passages are those where O'Casey relies on his native Irish-English vernacular, such as when the dry-land sailor Captain Boyle recalls his fabled past to his "butty" Joxer:

Them was days, Joxer, them was days. Nothin' was too hot or too heavy for me then. Sailin' from the Gulf o' Mexico to the Antanartic Ocean. I seen things, I seen things, Joxer, that no mortal man should speak about that knows his Catechism. Ofen, an' ofen, when I was fixed to the wheel with a marlinspike, an' the win's blowin' fierce an' the waves lashin' an' lashin', till you'd think every minute was goin' to be your last, an' it blowed, an' blowed—blew is the right word, Joxer, but blowed is what the sailors use . . .[18]

Unfortunately, we know very little about O'Casey's early attempts at writing plays, and that little through what he tells us in *Inishfallen Fare Thee Well*. Of the four early plays he mentions—*The Robe of Rosheen*, *The Frost in the Flower*, *The Harvest Festival*, and *The Crimson in the Tri-Colour*—not one has yet come to light. It is possible that they exist, for Joseph Holloway (a theatregoer noted for his voluminous diary *Impressions of a Dublin Playgoer*) writes of O'Casey having told him: "Fay wanted his earlier plays that were refused by the Abbey but he wouldn't give them to him or anyone. He said he destroyed them but he didn't. He hopes to use some of the dialogue later on."[19] O'Casey tells us that he incorporated a character from *The Crimson in the Tri-Colour* and a one-acter *The Cooing of Doves* (rejected by the Abbey Theatre a few months after the success of *The Shadow of a Gunman*) into his masterpiece *The Plough and the Stars*. Robert Hogan observes that *The Harvest Festival* contained the germ of his most recent long play, *The Drums of Father Ned*.[20]

Though O'Casey wrote his first play in 1911 for the Drama Club attached to the National Movement, it was not till after the Rising that he decided to offer a play to the Abbey management. The first play he sent to the theatre was called *The Frost in the Flower*, about 1919. It was a satire on a friend, Frank Cahill, and some leading members of the O'Toole Club. The play was returned to him with the remark: "Not far from being a good play." O'Casey followed up with another play called *The Harvest Festival*, which "dealt with the efforts

of militant members of the unskilled unions to put more
of the fibre of resistance to evil conditions of pay and
life into the hearts and minds of the members of the
craft unions whose gospel was that what was good
enough for the fathers was good enough for the sons."[21]
The play came back with a letter saying "that the work
was well conceived, but badly executed."[22] The third
play, *The Crimson in the Tri-Colour*, which dealt with the
tussle between Labour and the Sinn Fein, was also
returned, but not before hope was raised in the author
that it might be accepted. Both Lady Gregory and
Lennox Robinson liked the play in parts, Lady Gregory
telling the author: "I believe there is something in you
and your strong point is characterisation."[23] This advice,
coupled with Yeats's exhortation to O'Casey to write of
the life he knew, resulted a year later in *The Shadow of
a Gunman*—a play that was immediately accepted.

REFERENCES

1. *G.C.*, p. 213. See also *P.H.*, p. 57.
2. *I.F.T.W.*, p. 287.
3. *I.K.D.*, p. 37.
4. *I.K.D.*, p. 154.
5. Cowasjee, p. 36.
6. *Red Roses for Me*, p. 135.
7. *I.K.D.*, p. 207.
8. G. Fallon, "The House on the North Circular Road," *Modern Drama*, 4, Dec. 1961, p. 229.
9. *D.U.W.*, pp. 190-1.
10. *F.G.C.*, p. 43.
11. *F.G.C.*, p. 44.
12. *F.G.C.*, p. xii.
13. *F.G.C.*, p. xiii.
14. *F.G.C.*, p. xii.
15. *F.G.C.*, p. 1.
16. *F.G.C.*, pp. 69-71.
17. *J.P.*, pp. 54-5.
18. *J.P.*, p. 26.
19. MS. 1886, Apr.-Jun. 1924, p. 1041.
20. *F.G.C.*, p. 271.
21. *I.F.T.W.*, p. 119.
22. *I.F.T.W.*, p. 119.
23. *Lady Gregory's Journals*, 1946, p. 73.

CHAPTER II

THE DUBLIN PLAYS

In April 1923, the Abbey Theatre produced *The Shadow of a Gunman*: the first of O'Casey's famous Dublin trilogy; the other two plays being *Juno and the Paycock* (1925) and *The Plough and the Stars* (1926). The three plays have many features in common. They have a war period for background, and O'Casey views the war strictly from the angle of the slum dweller. Though "O'Casey is in the main a war dramatist,"[1] in these plays he condemns all wars and shows their horrible impact on the people who have the least to do with fighting. Tenement life is depicted with great realism and accuracy. Characters generally take precedence over plot: in the main his women are brave and earthy, his men are dreamers and braggarts. Though the plays are conceived as tragedies, the comedy element dominates and they can with greater accuracy be described as tragi-comedies. O'Casey's attitude towards the Church, a vital factor in Irish life and one that was to occupy him a great deal later on, is not clearly defined, nor is his interest in Communism. His main concern is to portray the lives of the poor and he does so in the sharp outline possible only for a man who has lived and loved and suffered among his people.

Before coming to the plays, one point needs to be stressed: these plays are intensely Irish and a knowledge of the times in which they are set is essential for a proper understanding of them. It was the audiences' lack of understanding of the political background to *The Shadow of a Gunman*, rather than the play's very obvious

flaws, which was responsible for the cold reception given
it at the Court Theatre, London, and the Goodman
Memorial Theatre, Chicago. The Dublin plays should
be read in conjunction with O'Casey's autobiographies,
for these dramas are chronicles of his life and of the
darkest period in his country's history. A careful reading
of the autobiographies will reveal that the same technique, the same concern, and the same scenes govern all
his works. The autobiographies also give a clue to
O'Casey's fondness for melodrama.

In O'Casey's early plays, melodrama is often used to
usher in some of his most poignant moments. But apart
from this, melodrama has a place in its own right: it is
a part of the times he is dramatising, as is borne out by
his autobiographies. Tragi-comedy may or may not be
the "highest form" of drama, but it is nearer life than
either pure comedy or pure tragedy. Techniques and
rules are not O'Casey's concern and have never been in
his whole dramatic career; his aim is to give an honest
and unflinching portrayal of his countrymen and times.
And that he does so has never been seriously questioned
even by his most vehement critics. It is no exaggeration
to say that the trilogy is a suitable appendix to any
political and social history of Ireland between the years
1916 and 1923.

The Shadow of a Gunman concerns a pseudo-poet Donal
Davoren, who is suffering the company of his pedlar
friend, Seumas Shields, in a tenement room. Davoren's
attempt to compose poetry is continually interrupted by
the idle chatter of his companions and the numerous
invasions of the room by the other residents of the house.
There is a visit from Maguire, a supposed pedlar, who
leaves a bag behind; then from the landlord, for long
overdue rent. When these people leave and there is
hope that now Davoren may be able to summon up his
muse, the pretty Minnie Powell comes in for a little milk
to colour her tea. She loves Davoren, because she thinks

him a "gunman" and a poet; Davoren welcomes her, for she is infinitely better company than his troublesome neighbours. A tender and humorous love scene is cut short by the intrusion of the bragging Tommy Owens, and of Mrs Henderson and Mr Gallogher. They, like Minnie Powell, believe the poet to be a gunman.

The second act—it is night now—brings none of the peace and quietness which Davoren is seeking. In rushes Mrs Grigson to complain that her husband has not yet returned from the snugs, to be followed by the boastful Mr Grigson himself. Minutes later the Black and Tans raid the house. The bag which Maguire had left is found to contain bombs, and Minnie out of her love for Davoren takes them to her room. She is discovered in possession of bombs and shot "while attempting to escape"[2] (an excuse, as every Irishman then knew, for being shot arbitrarily). Davoren, horror-stricken, bemoans the death of Minnie in a cry more poetic (there is in it the echo of Ecclesiastes XII. 6) than anything he has composed so far: "Oh, Donal Davoren, shame is your portion now till the silver cord is loosened and the golden bowl be broken."[3]

The play has a weak plot. Robert Hogan in his detailed analysis of it rightly observes that "O'Casey employs characters demanded only by the mechanics rather than by the essence of the plot."[4] In Act I, to keep the plot moving, he introduces Tommy Owens, Mr Mulligan, Mrs Henderson and Mr Gallogher. But none of these characters appears in Act II; on the other hand, two new characters, Mr and Mrs Grigson, are introduced at this late stage. The Grigsons are necessary to the play, but they should have been introduced earlier and substituted for Mrs Henderson and Mr Gallogher, if these last two had any purpose in the play besides extending the scene.

The need to introduce numerous characters arose because O'Casey had spread material suitable for a one-act play over two acts. The whole play centres on the raid—a raid that had to come as a surprise. Now a raid is a thing that acquires strength from being brief, and though O'Casey was as yet an inexperienced dramatist he knew this. There was just one thing he could have done: written a one-act play. Had he done so, he could have speeded up the action, got rid of the unnecessary characters, and worked the play steadily to its logical climax. It would then have attained the unity it now so sadly lacks.

In spite of serious flaws, *The Shadow of a Gunman* is still good drama. The critic of *The Times* (London) commenting on it, said: "Yet this is a play that neither an unimaginative audience nor inadequate acting can suppress. Mr. O'Casey has poured into this description of a night of terror in a Dublin tenement during 'the troubles' enough drama and enough thrilling emotion to supply half a dozen of our usual plays."[5] There are many fine touches: the sudden entry and exit of Maguire is effective; it creates both uneasiness and suspense in the mind of the audience. Tommy Owen preventing Davoren from kissing Minnie "is shrewd stagecraft, because nothing is quite so frequently deathly as a stage kiss, and also because few devices increase the tension of a play as well as a kiss deferred."[6] But the finest thing in the play is O'Casey's handling of the raid. In a scene that lasts less than ten minutes, O'Casey has captured the brutality of the Black and Tans during their year and a half's reign in Ireland.

O'Casey's great gift is characterisation. The characters in this play are not as sharply etched as in the other two Dublin plays, but they ring true and are drawn from the people he knew intimately. Moreover, *The Shadow of a Gunman* is the most autobiographical of all his plays. The raid that he has depicted actually took place while he was staying with a friend, Mícheál Ó Maoláin, at 35 Mountjoy Square (in the play he refers to it as

Hilljoy Square), in May 1920. O'Casey has written about the raid in *Inishfallen Fare Thee Well* and it is worth comparing the account given in the autobiography with that in the play. Ó Maoláin too has written about the raid in *Feasta* under the title "An Ruathar Úd Agus A nDeachaigh Leis." The description he gives of the room with its two windows, a stretcher bed, etc., tallies with O'Casey's description of the room in the play. The only fictitious thing in the story is Maguire leaving a bag full of bombs in Davoren's room. Actually, O'Casey had in his possession the reports of the I.C.A., and the fear of the Black and Tans discovering this terrified both him and Ó Maoláin.

In portraying Davoren, O'Casey has drawn on that part of his own character that he wishes to ridicule. Note O'Casey's description of him and see how closely it fits the dramatist himself:

There is in his face an expression that seems to indicate an eternal war between weakness and strength; there is in the lines of the brow and chin an indication of a desire for activity, while in his eyes there is visible an unquenchable tendency towards rest. His struggle through life has been a hard one . . . . His life would drive him mad were it not for the fact that he never knew any other. He bears upon his body the marks of the struggle for existence and the effort towards self-expression.[7]

Strangely, there is little indication in the play that Davoren has lived a hard life! Seumas Shields, the cowardly and voluble pedlar, is a caricature of Ó Maoláin. Minnie Powell, the brave girl for whom love is greater than the Republic, has her realistic basis in many young women in Ireland who fought for Ireland's freedom; perhaps in Linda Kearns who was sentenced to ten years' imprisonment for carrying ammunition. Maguire, the man of much action but few words, is possibly modelled on a Seumas McGowin who once belonged to the Citizen Army; and Adolphus Grigson, the first of O'Casey's brilliant braggarts, was in real life a printer's compositor.

To my mind the most accurate summing up of the play is by Ivor Brown when he says: "Infirmity of hand there may be, but infirmity of purpose there certainly is not."[8] O'Casey's purpose is to give a faithful picture of tenement life and the chaotic condition to which Ireland had been reduced. During the day the people live in filth, squalor, ugliness; there is no privacy, and great fear of being ejected by the landlords, who are interested in their rent and nothing else. During the night they lie awake, praying and hoping that there will be no raid, no death. As for the state of Ireland, the conversation between Davoren and Seumas tells us more than we may like to know:

SEUMAS: I wish to God it was all over. The country is gone mad. Instead of counting their beads now they're countin' bullets; their Hail Marys and paternosters are burstin' bombs—burstin' bombs, an' the rattle of machine-guns; petrol is their holy water; their Mass is a burnin' buildin'; their De Profundis is "The Soldiers' Song", an' their creed is, I believe in the gun almighty, maker of heaven an' earth—an' it's all for "the glory o' God an' the honour o' Ireland".

DAVOREN: I remember the time when you yourself believed in nothing but the gun.

SEUMAS: Ay, when there wasn't a gun in the country; I've a different opinion now when there's nothin' but guns in the country. . . . An' you daren't open your mouth, for Kathleen ni Houlihan is very different now to the woman who used to play the harp an' sing "Weep on, weep on, your hour is past", for she's a ragin' divil now, an' if you only look crooked at her you're sure of a punch in th' eye. But this is the way I look at it—I look at it this way: You're not goin'

—you're not goin' to beat the British Empire—the British Empire, by shootin' an occasional Tommy at the corner of an occasional street. Besides, when the Tommies have the wind up—when the Tommies have the wind up they let bang at everything they see— they don't give a God's curse who they plug.

DAVOREN: Maybe they ought to get down off the lorry and run to the Records Office to find out a man's pedigree before they plug him.

SEUMAS: It's the civilians that suffer; when there's an ambush they don't know where to run. Shot in the back to save the British Empire, an' shot in the breast to save the soul of Ireland. I'm a Nationalist meself, right enough—a Nationalist right enough, but all the same—I'm a Nationalist right enough; I believe in the freedom of Ireland, an' that England has no right to be here, but I draw the line when I hear the gunmen blowin' about dyin' for the people, when it's the people that are dyin' for the gunmen! With all due respect to the gunmen, I don't want them to die for me.[9]

Where else but in this play do we have the Dublin of 1920 with all its terror? Where else is the tragedy of the poor better captured than in the anxious concern of Mrs Grigson for her husband's safety, or is it her own? It's curfew hour and Mr Grigson has not yet returned from the snugs. What is she to do? What if anything should happen to him? "Not that I'd be any the worse if anything did happen to him," Mrs Grigson admits; but still: "Do the insurance companies pay if a man's is shot after curfew?"[10] In two sentences O'Casey has told us more about the poor than his fellow dramatists have done in whole acts. In the next two plays his concern for the poor becomes even more manifest, and he views the Irish struggle for freedom and the resultant bloodshed strictly from the angle of the tenement dweller.

Juno and the Paycock, which to English audiences is

O'Casey's most popular play, has for its background
the Civil War between the Irishmen who supported the
Free State and the Republicans who rejected it. So much
has been made of the brutalities committed by the
English in the Easter Rising and the Anglo-Irish Wars
both of which preceded the Civil War, that the atrocious
killing of Irishmen by Irishmen is sometimes forgotten.
Arland Ussher tells us of a leader boasting that the men
in arms against the Free State in Dublin numbered more
than the total in the whole country who fought against
the British, and goes on to add: "In the end this aimless
blood-lust seemed to communicate itself to the government side; seventy-seven of the Republican leaders were
executed—a total compared with which General
Maxwell's fifteen in Easter Week seems a mere *hors
d'oeuvre*—but this time the weary population did not put
the heroes' photographs on post-cards."[11] To O'Casey
all killing was bad, and it little mattered whether a
fellow was shot in the front or in the back, or whether
the killer was an Englishman or an Irishman.

The play concerns the Boyle family who are trapped
between events they themselves have precipitated and
others over which they have no control. While Jack
Boyle, the dry-land sailor, struts about the snugs satura-
ting himself on stout with his "butty" Joxer, Juno Boyle,
his sharp-tongued but hard-working wife, keeps the
home together. Their daughter, Mary, stays home
on strike and their son, Johnny, invalided in the Easter
Rising, haunts their two-roomed dwelling. The family
is on the verge of financial collapse when the news of
an unexpected legacy is brought by the school-teacher
Bentham, to whom Mary has given her love after rejecting
the advances of the Labour leader, Jerry Devine. On
the strength of this windfall the dingy rooms are decor-
ated and the neighbours entertained. But tragedy moves
in swiftly: Mary is left pregnant by her suitor Bentham,
the promise of the will is not fulfilled and their debts

ave mounted, and Johnny is taken out and shot for
etraying a comrade. Juno and Mary leave the house,
nd the curtain comes down on the drunken Captain
s he totters in unmindful of his son's death, his daughter's
light, and his wife's desertion.

Juno and the Paycock is much better constructed than
The Shadow of a Gunman, though a few critics have com-
lained about its structural faults. One criticism frequently made against the play is that it lacks unity. Mr
Milton Waldman writes:

> There are thus three lines of plot, the Boyles' elusive in-
> heritance, Mary's unfortunate love affair, and Johnny's
> treachery. Neither of the former two has any relation
> to the last, and their connection with each other is,
> to say the least, slender.[12]

Now these three lines of plot are related, not in any
scene or incident but in a character—Juno Boyle. It is
Juno's tragedy that the "Paycock," living on an imaginary nautical prestige, should drink himself into debt,
that Mary should be seduced and then deserted by a
worthless liar, that Johnny should be led to his death
for betraying a friend. The play is brought to its focal
point in the character of Juno.

There is much that is admirable in O'Casey's handling
of the plot. The opening scene is perfect, and Lennox
Robinson praises it discriminatingly:

> In five minutes or so, Seán O'Casey has "planted"
> four of the chief protagonists in his drama. Nothing
> they do or say is extraneous to the plot. We get his
> scene, a slum room (producer's business and wardrobe-
> mistress's and property-man's), we get that the scene
> is laid in Dublin by the accent of the players (players'
> business); we get Juno's character, worried over her
> thriftless husband but a good anxious mother; we get
> Mary, a little vain, a little selfish; we get Johnny, we

suspect something from his nervousness, his reaction to the reading of the details of the assassination; we get vigorous young Jerry Devine; we have talked about the Paycock and his wastrel friend Joxer—though we have not yet seen them their shadows have already fallen quite distinctly across the play—and all this has been done in a few minutes of superb stage-craft.[13]

Among other scenes and incidents judiciously handled there are those which centre on Johnny Boyle: th character that links the Boyle tragedy with the Civi War. Carefully and gradually O'Casey reveals Johnny betrayal of a friend. Not till the end of the second ac are we certain what is weighing on Johnny's mind. Ha O'Casey revealed Johnny's disloyalty earlier than h does in the play, we would certainly have failed to enjo the scene where the Boyles luxuriate in the prospect o the elusive legacy. Again, consider how in the final ac O'Casey prevents Mary and Boyle from confrontin each other. Boyle is righteously indignant about Mary pregnancy, but a scene in which the two are brough face to face would deprive Boyle of some of his ga feathers. Besides, it would make his hypocrisy intoler able.[14] Instead O'Casey lets Johnny abuse Mary. W cannot miss the irony, for Johnny himself is guilty of . far more serious lapse than his sister.

The finest thing in the play is the drunken frolickin of Boyle and Joxer, which immediately follows its mos tragic moment: Johnny's death and Juno's great prayer Robert Hogan has called it "one of the most devastatin moments of the modern drama,"[15] and Micheá MacLiammóir writes:

Few moments on any stage can have impressed as that when Juno hears that her daughter is going to have a child; few moments have existed for me of such torn and conflicting emotions as when the two drunken

pals come staggering back to the darkened room,
knowing nothing of what has passed, and still dreaming
of a bright, Christmas-number, temperance-magazine
Ireland, sober and free and innocent of baleful
tempters and scarlet sins, while the ruined boards
creak under their feet and one can almost hear the
plaster falling from the desiccated ceiling.[16]

There are some who feel that this scene should have been
omitted altogether, and others that it should have been
briefer. There is nothing to warrant either of these sug-
gestions. Not only do we have here the most magnificent
juxtaposition of tragedy and comedy, but the entire piece
is an integral part of the theme: to show how men escape
their sorrows while the women toil under them. Slum
life has its own humour, tragic though it may well be.
With tear-blinded eyes we watch the drunken entry of
the "Paycock," to give ourselves away to uncontrollable
laughter as he subsides in a sitting posture on the floor
and attributes the present state of affairs to a world in
disorder: "I'm telling you . . . Joxer . . . th' whole
worl's . . . in a terr . . . ible state o' . . . chassis!"[17]

The characterisation, too, is much richer than in the
previous play. All the major characters are drawn from
people O'Casey knew, and in the case of Captain Boyle
and Joxer Daly* he did not even change their names.
These two characters provide the best part of the comedy
in the play. They are neither fools nor knaves; both have
an ingenious sense of self-preservation and a sound
understanding of each other's character. But hard times
have brought them together: Boyle needs an audience
for his tales of imaginary escapades, and Joxer a "cup

---

*Mr Jack Daly, whom I have quoted on pp. xi and 59 of my
study *Sean O'Casey: the Man Behind the Plays*, should not be confused
with Jack (Joxer) Daly, the inseparable snug-mate of Captain Jack
Boyle. If I have given my readers the impression that the two Dalys
are one and the same person, I am sorry.

C

o' tay." These are the facts, and the rest is fiction. Joxer can start the Captain off on his long voyage from "the Gulf o' Mexico to the Antarctic Ocean" by recalling: "God be with the young days when you were steppin' the deck of a manly ship, with the win' blowin' a hurricane through the masts, an' the only sound you'd hear was, 'Port your helm!' an' the only answer, 'Port it is, sir!' "[18] He can a few minutes later lay bare Boyle's naked self by asserting: "I have to laugh every time I look at the deep-sea sailor; an' a row on a river ud make him sea-sick!"[19] But what difference does that make? Boyle remains true to his world of fantasy. One cannot but envy his splendid audacity: his ability to believe in himself and his fake heroics in the face of so much adverse evidence.

Juno, the greatest of O'Casey's heroines, has often been referred to as the greatest mother in drama. In the midst of shirkers, braggarts, the wrong-principled and the good-for-nothings, she alone shows courage and common sense. In scene after scene her hard grasp of the facts of life is brought into contrast with the stupid idealism of her daughter and son and the dream world of her husband.

> MARY: What's the use of belongin' to a Trades Union if you won't stand up for your principles? Why did they sack her? It was a clear case of victimization. We couldn't let her walk the streets, could we?
> MRS BOYLE: No, of course yous couldn't—yous wanted to keep her company. Wan victim wasn't enough. When the employers sacrifice wan victim, the Trades Unions go wan betther be sacrificin' a hundred.[20]

It is not that Juno is against trade unions but that she is for the workers earning their daily bread. Nor is she against Irish freedom, but against war and brutal killing. When Johnny, who has already earned a shattered hip and lost an arm, boasts that he is prepared to make the same sacrifice again for Ireland's sake, for "a principle's a principle," she wisely remarks: "Ah, you lost your best principle, me boy, when you lost your arm; them's the only sort o' principles that's any good to a workin' man."[21]

Courage and common sense never forsake Juno, not even in the most tragic moment of the play: when she gets the news of Johnny's death.

> MARY: Oh, it's thrue, it's thrue what Jerry Devine says—there isn't a God, there isn't a God; if there was He wouldn't let these things happen!
> MRS BOYLE: Mary, Mary, you mustn't say them things. We'll want all the help we can get from God an' His Blessed Mother now! These things have nothin' to do with the Will o' God. Ah, what can God do agen the stupidity o' men![22]

Mary puts down the sorrow that visits her to the absence of Providence, Johnny to his principles, and the "Paycock" to a world in chaos. Only Juno faces reality and puts the blame squarely on mankind. This is highly significant. There may be no reforming zeal as such in these early plays, but Joseph Wood Krutch is wide of the mark when he asserts that O'Casey "offers no solution; he proposes no remedy; he suggests no hope."[23] As long as there are people like Juno, there is sanity. And in sanity there is both hope and remedy.

If *Juno and the Paycock* brought Dublin to O'Casey's feet, *The Plough and the Stars* set the Dubliners kicking. The play had aroused some apprehension at the Abbey as soon as it was received. Mr George O'Brien, a Government nominee and the only Catholic Director on the Theatre's Board, took objection to the introduction of the prostitute, Rosie Redmond, in the play and the emphasis given to her "professional" side; Michael Dolan, the Theatre's Manager, objected to the play's

language and described it as "beyond the beyonds";
the actress Eileen Crowe, who was to play Mrs Gogan,
refused to utter the lines "Ne'er a one o' Jennie Gogan's
kids was born outside of th' bordhers of the Ten Com-
mandments";[24] and the actor F. J. McCormick refused
to speak the word "Snotty." Yeats and Lady Gregory
stood firmly behind the play, refusing to sacrifice
artistic principles to puritanical considerations. Lady
Gregory made her position clear: "If we have to choose
between the subsidy"—the theatre just then had been
granted an annual subsidy by the Irish government—
"and our freedom, it is our freedom we choose."[52] However, adjustments had to be made: Rosie Redmond's
song and certain lines to which Dolan had objected were
removed. Still the actors refused to swing themselves
into the drama.

The play had its premiere at the Abbey Theatre on
8 Feb. 1926. On the first night it received a great ovation;
there were signs of restlessness in the audience on the
next two nights; and on the fourth night riots broke out,
police were called in, and the play progressed in pande-
monium. Yeats, who had anticipated this and was eager
to teach the Dubliners a lesson, rushed on to the stage
and delivered his famous oration, which is to-day as
familiar to students of Irish drama as Lincoln's Gettysberg
oration is to students of American history:

I thought you had got tired of all this which com-
menced about fifteen years ago [the riots over the
performance of *The Playboy of the Western World* in
1907]. But you have disgraced yourselves again. Is
this to be an ever recurring celebration of the arrival
of Irish genius? Synge first and then O'Casey. The
news of the happenings of the last few minutes will go
from country to country. Dublin has once more
rocked the cradle of a reputation. From such a scene
in this theatre went forth the fame of Synge. Equally

the fame of O'Casey is born here tonight. This is his apotheosis.[26]

There were no further incidents of rioting on the following nights, not because of Yeats's sermon but because of the general realisation that O'Casey's portrayal, though it might not be complimentary to the Irish, was nevertheless true. However, certain Irish writers and critics who disliked O'Casey made good use of this opportunity to denigrate him. The novelist Liam O'Flaherty described *The Plough and the Stars* as a bad play; the poet F. R. Higgins wrote:

A new political quality approved by the arrogance of the Anglo-Irish is the only quality for which O'Casey is offered applause. His is a technique based on the revue structure, in the quintessence of an all-Abbey burlesque, intensified by "diversions" and Handy Andy incidents, with somewhat more original settings. O'Casey in his new plays entirely lacks the sincerity of the artist.

Mr R. M. Fox referred to the play as "The Drama of the Dregs," and said: "The peasant plays have been followed by slum plays, but their reign will not be long, though as entertainment these slum dramas are permissible. But truth is wanted as well as entertainment."[27] There was so much truth in the play that it quickly expelled the malicious criticism heaped on it and established for itself a popularity in Dublin that remains unchallenged.

The public rioted because O'Casey had defended the innocent victims of the Rising rather than the heroes; he had brought their tri-colour into a pub; he had introduced a prostitute in the second act, and had ridiculed the men who had laid down their lives in Easter Week. To-day these may seem puerile reasons for rioting, but in a country that had just regained freedom after 700 years of struggle, feeling ran high. Also, let us not forget what two well-known English critics could say even of a play like *Juno and the Paycock*, which the Dubliners accepted with cheers. Ivor Brown wrote: "Dublin has seen this play [*Juno and the Paycock*], I believe, without much protest, though it is twenty times as strong an accusation as ever lay beneath the laughter of Synge";[28] and Desmond MacCarthy exclaimed: "This play, thank God, is not about us."[29] The American critic G. J. Nathan showed surprise not at the Irishmen rioting over *The Plough and the Stars*, but at what they could tolerate:

> As a surgical picture of the Irish, I know of nothing in drama or literature that comes anywhere near this play. That the Irish merely gave vent to catcalls and eggs when it was shown in Dublin is surprising; that they didn't bomb the theatre is even more surprising. O'Casey takes his people, themselves, their ambitions, their pretences, and their innermost philosophies, and doesn't leave a green thread in their chemises when he gets through.[30]

O'Casey defended himself with all the facts at his disposal. In two letters, both written in reply to the accusations of Mrs Sheehy-Skeffington (wife of the pacifist Francis Skeffington, who was shot by mistake in the Easter Rising), he pointed out that he himself had seen the tri-colour brought into a public house; more, he had seen it painted on a lavatory door. He also defended his portrayal of Nora Clitheroe, the heroine who is only concerned with the safety of her husband, saying: "Nora voices not only the feeling of Ireland's women, but the women of the human race. The safety of her brood is the true morality of every woman."[31] O'Casey was, however, wrong in saying "There isn't a coward in the play."[32] What is Peter Flynn if not a coward? What may be said with greater accuracy is that in the play there is not a single male character who is really brave and unselfish. And in the Easter Rising there were brave men, few though they might be.

The Plough and the Stars is about the tenement dwellers caught in the Easter Rising. Jack Clitheroe, a bricklayer, goes out to fight for freedom, but not till he is made Commandant. Nora, his affectionate wife, stays at home worrying over her husband's safety. The other tenement dwellers, when they are not looting, sit around cursing, gambling, swearing, applauding the fighters from a safe distance, and keeping out of harm's way. The result is not far from what one would expect: Clitheroe is killed, Nora goes insane, and a couple of characters that had the least to do with the Rising are dead. But the braggarts and the good-for-nothings live on.

The plot of *The Plough and the Stars* has invited diverse opinions. Allardyce Nicoll and Andrew Malone feel that the play has no plot; Brooks Atkinson feels that the plot needs compression; Robert Hogan thinks it "the most cunningly contrived and greatest achievement of O'Casey's early period."[33] Between these extremes stands Padraic Colum's balanced judgment: "Considering the mass of things that are involved in it, the action of 'The Plough and the Stars' is compact and well ordered."[34] It is very easy to talk of the lack of unity in a play whose subject is so broad and so detailed, where in theory the protagonists of the drama are Jack and Nora but in essence they are the Dublin tenement dwellers: shiftless of character and romantic of temperament, who preferred cheering rebels to fighting in their company.

The first two acts are set in November 1915 and the last two acts in the Easter Week of 1916. The first act is given primarily to introducing the characters and setting the play in motion. It opens with Mrs Gogan, a charwoman who takes a macabre delight in deaths and funerals, complaining to Fluther Good when she sees the new hat that has arrived for Nora Clitheroe: "God, she's goin' to th' divil lately for style! That hat, now, costs more than a penny."[35] O'Casey wishes to show here that the opposition the women meet in their attempt to improve their lot comes not only from men alone (in fact in the Dublin plays the men are too occupied with their dreams to look to their homes) but from other women as well. In *The Shadow of a Gunman*, Minnie is criticised for her "fancy stockins an' her pompoms an her crêpe de chine blouses"; in *Juno and the Paycock*, Juno upbraids Mary for her concern over ribbons; and in this play we see Mrs Gogan, and the fruit-vendor, Bessie Burgess, hammering out at Nora's constant concern for "respectability." Undoubtedly, O'Casey's sympathies lie with his women. But he is too great an artist to gloss over their faults.

O'Casey's three braggarts next invade the stage, and though the scenes that follow consist mostly of knock-about farce which takes us nowhere, we get to know the people who actually decided the outcome of Easter Week. The greatest character here is Fluther Good, a carpenter, fashioned on a Falstaffian scale. Holloway tells us that Fluther Good's real name was John Good, but that he got the name of Fluther by hitting a street-musician (a flautist) on the head with his own instrument.[36] David Krause describes him as a "knight-errant of the tenements," one whose "roar is worse than his bite; he starts more arguments than he can settle; he rages and boasts, lies and threatens when he is cornered; he swears abstinence then drowns himself in drink when the shops are looted, crying 'Up the Rebels' and 'th' whole city can topple home to hell' in the same drunken breath; he can defend a prostitute's good name, and then go off to spend the night with her."[37] The Covey, a cousin of Clitheroe, is a sham communist harping on socialism, which he understands as little as anybody else in the play. Peter Flynn, Nora's uncle, is the source of much amusement. Dressed in the green and gold uniform of the Foresters, he spends the best part of his time cursing and swearing at the Covey. O'Casey, as secretary of the Irish Citizen Army, favoured guerilla warfare and was against the wearing of uniforms, since these would only give the fighters away to the enemy. It is no accident that in the last act Captain Brennan has to get into civvies to escape the English.

The play gains momentum with the entry of Clitheroe, who has lost interest in the Citizen Army because he has not been made a captain. A tender love scene between Clitheroe and Nora comes to an abrupt conclusion when Clitheroe learns that Nora has burned the letter from General Connolly appointing him commandant. As he walks out to assume command of his battalion, the unhappy Nora speaks bitterly: "Your vanity'll be th' ruin of you an' me yet. . . . That's what's movin' you: because they've made an officer of you, you'll make a glorious cause of what you're doin'."[38] We soon discover the truth in Nora's outburst.

Yeats called the second act of *The Plough and the Stars* "the finest O'Casey has written." O'Casey makes his *mise en scène* a local bar, not only because of the significant part pubs have played in Irish life but also because it is the one place where characters from all walks of life can assemble, be they visionaries, rogues, cowards, or prostitutes. Visible from time to time through the window is the silhouette of a man outside preaching to the crowd his gospel of war and the self-purification by blood sacrifice. Inside the pub there are Fluther, Peter Flynn, the Covey, Mrs Gogan, and Bessie Burgess, drinking as a matter of urgent duty and hurling invective at each other. There is also the prostitute Rosie Redmond, regretting that the meeting has put the people in a "holy mood" and so deprived her of a day's business. The normal grossness of life inside the pub is brought into painful contrast with the high idealism of the Speaker and his impassioned call for duty and heroism. The more sacrifice the Speaker demands, the less the pub's inmates are willing to give. The inverse ratio is carefully proportioned and is worth examining in some detail.

The four passages declaimed by the Speaker are adapted from the speeches of Padraic Pearse, Commander of the Irish Volunteers in the Easter Rising. The first runs:

> It is a glorious thing to see arms in the hands of Irishmen. We must accustom ourselves to the thought of arms, we must accustom ourselves to the sight of arms, we must accustom ourselves to the use of arms. . . . Bloodshed is a cleansing and sanctifying thing, and the nation that regards it as the final horror has lost its manhood. . . . There are many things more horrible than bloodshed, and slavery is one of them![39]

To this speech both Fluther and Peter react with excessive emotional fervency, Peter claiming that "A meetin' like this always makes me feel as if I could dhrink Loch Erinn dhry!"[40] and Fluther responding that that is the right sort of feeling. As they hurriedly gulp down their drinks and indulge in maudlin patriotism, the Speaker is seen for the second time:

> Comrade soldiers of the Irish Volunteers and of the Citizen Army, we rejoice in this terrible war. The old heart of the earth needed to be warmed with the red wine of the battlefields. . . . Such august homage was never offered to God as this: the homage of millions of lives given gladly for love of country. And we must be ready to pour out the same red wine in the same glorious sacrifice, for without shedding of blood there is no redemption![41]

The speech has a special significance to a predominantly Catholic audience, because of its allusions to the doctrine of Transubstantiation and the redemption through blood sacrifice. Its impact however is different: Fluther

and Peter rush out, Fluther exclaiming that "this is too
good to be missed!" The Covey comes in and Rosie
tries to entice him, but with no success. Fluther and
Peter reappear, followed by Mrs Gogan, but they no
longer talk of the meeting. The Bible-quoting Bessie
Burgess joins them a few minutes later. Soon the two
women are cursing and caluminating each other; the
Covey in the meantime has his jibe at Peter. In the midst
of this meaningless bickering, the Speaker is seen for
the third time:

> The last sixteen months have been the most glorious
> in the history of Europe. Heroism has come back to
> the earth. War is a terrible thing, but war is not an
> evil thing. People in Ireland dread war because they
> do not know it. Ireland has not known the exhilaration
> of war for a hundred years. When war comes to Ire-
> land she must welcome it as she would welcome the
> Angel of God![42]

The Covey calls it all "dope" and Fluther for the moment
has no comment to make. His enthusiasm for the fight
has been transmuted by strong drink. The two women's
ironic response to this call of duty is a preparation for
a fist fight, at which the barman throws them out. This
is followed by a heated exchange of words between
Fluther and the Covey; not because of the Covey's
contemptuous remarks about Ireland's struggle for
freedom, but because he has insulted a prostitute. The
barman pushes the Covey out, and the voice of the
Speaker is heard for the last time:

> Our foes are strong, but strong as they are, they
> cannot undo the miracles of God, who ripens in the
> heart of young men the seeds sown by the young men
> of a former generation. They think they have pacified
> Ireland, think they have foreseen everything; think
> they have provided against everything; but the fools,
> the fools, the fools!—they have left us our Fenian

dead, and, while Ireland holds these graves, Ireland, unfree, shall never be at peace![43]

To this speech there are two different sets of responses. The first is from Captain Brennan, Lieutenant Langon, and Clitheroe, who have just come into the bar and are in a state of high emotional excitement. They affirm their readiness to lay down their lives for Ireland. The other is from Fluther, who totally disregards the exhortation of the Speaker and walks out with the prostitute Rosie. His initial enthusiasm for Ireland's freedom coldly contrasts with his present behaviour. Fluther's failure to support the freedom fighters is symbolic of the failure of the Dublin citizen to respond to the call of duty.

Special mention must be made of Rosie Redmond, the one character who throughout the play remains rooted in the facts and the needs of daily life and is not swayed by any idealistic nonsense. She takes no sides on political issues: but is concerned only for her customers and her trade. While she is with the barman she calls the speech "th' sacred truth," for that is how the barman feels and he may reward her with a glass of malt; the next moment she calls the fighters a "lot o' thricksters" and the freedom not "worth winnin' in a raffle," for she is seeking business with the cynical Covey. Among men and women full of frenzy and excitement, she is the only character who keeps a sense of reality: the "fifty-five shillin's a week for your keep an' laundhry, an' then taxin' you a quid for your room if you bring home a friend for th' night."[44]

Having given us the picture of the vain, boasting tenement heroes who leapt up to answer the call of war when it was nowhere near, O'Casey now turns to show us how they conducted themselves when the fighting began. The tension builds up remorselessly. The setting of the third act is the Clitheroe home. While Mrs Gogan attends to her sick child Mollser, Fluther comes in

carrying Nora, who has been rushing round the barri-
cades looking for her husband.

I could find him nowhere, Mrs. Gogan. None o' them
would tell me where he was. They told me I shamed
my husband an' th' women of Ireland be carryin' on
as I was. . . . They said th' women must learn to be
brave an' cease to be cowardly. . . . Me who risked
more for love than they would risk for hate.[45]

When Clitheroe comes in a few minutes later and learns
that Nora has been out searching for him he rebukes
her: "Are you goin' to turn all th' risks I'm takin' into
a laugh?"[46] We are immediately reminded of Nora's
remark when Clitheroe set out to fight, "Your vanity'll
be th' ruin of you an' me yet . . ." Which then is brave?
Nora who searches for her husband in the bullet-haunted
streets or Clitheroe who dies fighting?

The scene between Nora and Clitheroe is juxtaposed
sharply with the comedy scene showing the looting and
plunder. Arland Ussher writes that "The only people
who had been enthusiastic were the looters from the
Dublin slums, who carried home in triumph pianos and
gramophones on trolley-carts through streets a-buzz
with bullets."[47] And Denis Johnston describes an
incident (he has used the incident to conclude scene I
of his play *The Scythe and the Sunset*, 1958), which he says
has not been included in the lore of those Homeric times:

A very brave and romantic young man, by name
Joseph Plunkett, stepped out of the rebel stronghold
in the General Post Office and began to read the Proclamation of the Irish Republic to the assembled
citizens at the base of the Nelson Pillar. He had not
gone very far with the news when there was a crash of
broken glass from nearby, and the cry went up,
'They're looting Noblett's Toffee Shop.' With a
whoop of delight that far exceeded their enthusiasm

for the Republic, the sovereign people departed,
leaving young Plunkett to finish his proclamation to
the empty air.[48]

These two quotations, in addition to what O'Casey
himself has written about the looting and plundering
in *Inishfallen Fare Thee Well*, prove how accurate
O'Casey's depiction of the event in the play is. And i
may be for this reason that those who rioted over *Th
Plough and the Stars* did not choose this particular scene
as their target.

The Clitheroe home has been riddled with bullets
and O'Casey for the fourth act takes us to Bessie Burgess'
living-room. There is death everywhere: in the stree
outside and in the house. Nora has gone insane; Mollse
and Nora's still-born child lie in a coffin, and at the foo
of the coffin the riff-raff are playing cards. The humou
is macabre, possibly influenced by O'Casey's study o
Modern Irish which is noted for this quality.[49] Also
the alternation of tragedy and comedy is so rapid tha
one is left flabbergasted; no moods or emotions dominat
the mind, but the grimmest of irony. Here is how th
act opens:

> FLUTHER [*furtively peeping out of the window*]: Give them
> a good shuffling. . . . Th' sky's gettin' reddher an'
> reddher. . . . You'd think it was afire. . . . Half o' th'
> city must be burnin'. . . .
>
> THE COVEY [*placing the cards on the floor, after shuffling
> them*]: Come on, an' cut.
>
> [*Fluther comes over, sits on the floor, and cuts the cards.*
> THE COVEY [*having dealt the cards*]: Spuds up again.
>
> [*Nora moans feebly in room on left.*
> FLUTHER: There, she's at it again. She's been quiet
> for a long time, all th' same.
>
> THE COVEY: She was quiet before, sure, an' she broke
> out again worse than ever. . . . What was led that
> time?

PETER: Thray o' Hearts, Thray o' Hearts, Thray o' Hearts.

FLUTHER: It's damned hard lines to think of her dead-born kiddie lyin' there in th' arms o' poor little Mollser. Mollser snuffed it sudden too, afther all.

THE COVEY: Sure she never got any care. How could she get it, an' th' mother out day an' night lookin' for work, an' her consumptive husband leavin' her with a baby to be born before he died!

Voices in a lilting chant to the Left in a distant street. Red Cr . . . oss, Red Cr . . . oss! . . . Ambu . . . lance, Ambu . . . lance!

THE COVEY [*to Fluther*]: Your deal, Fluther.

FLUTHER [*shuffling and dealing the cards*]: It'll take a lot out o' Nora—if she'll ever be th' same.[50]

The play ends with the death of Bessie in her attempt to save Nora. The English soldiers sit down to drink the tea Nora had prepared and sing "Keep the 'owme fires burning." Outside the city burns. On this terrible note of irony O'Casey brings the curtain down; and though he went on to write many fine plays he never again sent the curtain up on anything so moving as this tenement tragedy.

REFERENCES

1. G. Wilson Knight, *The Golden Labyrinth*, 1962, p. 373.
2. See Dorothy Macardle, *The Irish Republic*, 1951, p. 355.
3. *S.G.*, pp. 156-7.
4. Hogan, p. 29.
5. *The Times* (London), 26 Jan. 1953.
6. Hogan, p. 32.
7. *S.G.*, pp. 93-4.
8. "Cautionary Tales," *The Saturday Review*, 143, 18 Jun. 1927, p. 938.
9. *S.G.*, pp. 131-2.
10. *S.G.*, pp. 136-7.
11. *The Face and Mind of Ireland*, 1950, pp. 65-6.
12. "The Chronicles," *The London Mercury*, 13, Feb. 1926, p. 442.
13. *Towards an Appreciation of the Theatre*, 1945, pp. 18-9.
14. V. Mercier, *The Irish Comic Tradition*, 1962, p. 240.
15. Hogan, p. 41.
16. "Problem Plays," *The Irish Theatre*, ed. L. Robinson, 1939, p. 225.
17. *J.P.*, p. 89.

18. *J.P.*, pp. 25-6.
19. *J.P.*, p. 34.
20. *J.P.*, p. 6.
21. *J.P.*, p. 31.
22. *J.P.*, p. 86.
23. *"Modernism" in Modern Drama*, 1953, p. 99.
24. *I.F.T.W.*, p. 300.
25. *Lady Gregory's Journals*, 1946, p. 87.
26. Quoted in Cowasjee, p. 81.
27. *I.F.T.W.*, pp. 191-2.
28. "Life by the Liffey," *The Saturday Review*, 120, 21 Nov. 1925, p. 594.
29. "Juno and the Paycock," *The New Statesman*, 26, 28 Nov. 1925, p. 207.
30. *Art of the Night*, 1928, pp. 188-9.
31. "A Reply to the Critics," *The Irish Times*, 19 Feb. 1926.
32. *Irish Independent*, 23 Feb. 1926.
33. Hogan, p. 41.
34. *Saturday Review of Literature*, 2, 12 Jun. 1926, p. 854.
35. *P.S.*, p. 163.
36. MS. 1900, Jan.-Mar. 1926, p. 431.
37. Krause, p. 80.
38. *P.S.*, p. 189.
39. *P.S.*, pp. 193-4.
40. *P.S.*, p. 194.
41. *P.S.*, pp. 195-6.
42. *P.S.*, pp. 202-3.
43. *P.S.*, p. 213.
44. *P.S.*, p. 193.
45. *P.S.*, pp. 219-20.
46. *P.S.*, p. 235.
47. *The Face and Mind of Ireland*, 1950, p. 35.
48. *Radio Times*, 13 Sep. 1946.
49. See chapter "Macabre and Grotesque Humour in the Irish Tradition," in Vivian Mercier's *The Irish Comic Tradition*.
50. *P.S.*, pp. 240-1.

CHAPTER III

THE EXPERIMENTAL PLAYS

Though *The Plough and the Stars* was as much an advance on *Juno and the Paycock* as *Juno and the Paycock* was on *The Shadow of a Gunman*, a break in subject-matter, treatment, and technique seemed necessary. At least two critics on viewing *The Plough and the Stars* at the Fortune Theatre, London, regretted that O'Casey should repeat himself. One wrote that it is "disquieting that he [O'Casey] should do it all again so exactly," and went on to say: "The prayers, hymns, and funeral of 'Juno' were too closely copied in the new play; and the magnificent audacity of the two beer drinkers at the end of one play should never have been repeated in the two indifferent tea-drinkers of the other."[1] The other said:

> I do not care if Mr. O'Casey takes us no further than Phoenix Park, though I'll go with him gladly for the sake of his glorious racy wit to the Wicklow Mountains and the plains beyond, but come out of the tenement houses round the Four Courts of Dublin he must, or his limitations as a dramatist are defined for ever. In theory, nothing could be more admirable than that a writer should write of what he knows; in practice, particularly in stage practice, the thing becomes monotonous, and monotony is a vice.[2]

Realism had never strongly appealed to O'Casey in spite of the success and fame it had brought him. He wrote in the realistic manner because Lady Gregory and Yeats insisted and because the Dublin audiences took to it heartily. His very first play to be published, *The*

D

Robe of Rosheen (now lost), was according to him "in the 'first principle' of a fantasy."[3] His one-acter *Kathleen Listens In*, which followed *The Shadow of a Gunman* and which has appeared in print in *Feathers from the Green Crow*, was also a fantasy with symbolic characters. The play was not warmly received and O'Casey had no choice but to write in the manner that was acceptable to his audiences. *Juno and the Paycock* and *The Plough and the Stars* brought him financial security—it is said that these two plays at one time earned him as much as £200 a week—and gave him an opportunity to go his own way and experiment with new techniques. O'Casey was, as he bellowed abroad time and time again, an experimental dramatist. In *The Green Crow* he wrote: "Dramatists cannot go on imitating themselves, and, when they get tired of that, imitating others. They must change, must experiment, must develop their power, or try to, if the drama is to live."[4]

O'Casey's first great experiment was *The Silver Tassie* and its immediate result was his break with the Abbey Theatre and exile. I have treated all this in great detail in my *Sean O'Casey: the Man Behind the Plays*; here we shall touch only on the pertinent details. As an experimental dramatist what O'Casey most needed was a theatre where he could try out his experiments, but Yeats's criticism of the new play and O'Casey's reaction to it unfortunately deprived him of such an opportunity. From 1928 onwards his plays were, with one or two exceptions, published before they were produced, and some of them did not get a production for years after they were published. This accounts for some of the flaws in O'Casey's later works and makes his break with the Abbey Theatre a tragic episode. His Dublin plays were produced first and published later, and O'Casey after seeing his work performed was able to make the necessary alterations. How a dramatist gains from seeing his play on the stage is best illustrated by *The Bishop's*

Bonfire. When this was produced by Cyril Cusack at the Gaiety Theatre, Dublin, the critic of *Punch* attacked the scene in which Foorawn writes a long letter after she is shot by her lover. He wrote:

A little startling, but no more; one was fascinated that as she slithered to the ground she contrived to write so long a letter, confessing suicide, that it must have been written in shorthand.[5]

The criticism was to the point and O'Casey in the published version of the play reduced the letter to a sentence.

O'Casey left Dublin in March 1926. He initially came to London for a short visit on J. B. Fagan's request (*Juno and the Paycock* was being transferred from the Royalty Theatre to the Fortune Theatre and Fagan wanted O'Casey to give the play fresh publicity). But London soon won O'Casey over: he made friends with G. B. Shaw and Augustus John; he fell in love with a charming Dublin girl Eileen Carey, and they were married in September 1927. London was now to be his home and workshop. His choice, no doubt, was partly influenced by the hostility with which some Irish critics and fellow dramatists were to greet *The Plough and the Stars*. These very people had hailed him once, but that was before they could be sure that this strange hod-carrier would steal the stage from them. O'Casey's spectacular success had bred more enemies than friends; also, the frank manner in which he voiced his opinions had made things worse. A study of Holloway's diary for the period April 1924 to March 1926 reveals why O'Casey was becoming unpopular: he was openly expressing views on the works of other dramatists and criticising Abbey productions.

W. B. Yeats and Lady Gregory, both Directors of the Abbey Theatre, admired O'Casey's great dramatic gift and were anxious that the Abbey should have his new play. O'Casey sent them the play in late March 1928.

A month later came Yeats's famous letter of rejection as well as the less forcible outcries of Lennox Robinson (Robinson and Walter Starkie were the other two Directors on the Abbey board) and Lady Gregory. Yeats wrote:

I am sad and discouraged. You have no subject. You were interested in the Irish Civil War, and at every moment of those plays wrote out of your own amusement with life or your sense of its tragedy; you were excited, and we all caught your excitement; you were exasperated almost beyond endurance by what you had seen or heard as a man is by what happens under his window, and you moved us as Swift moved his contemporaries. But you are not interested in the Great War; you never stood on its battlefields or walked its hospitals, and so write out of your opinions. You illustrate those opinions by a series of almost unrelated scenes, as you might in a leading article; there is no dominating character, no dominating action, neither psychological unity nor unity of action, and your great power of the past has been the creation of some unique character who dominated all about him and was himself a main impulse in some action that filled the play from beginning to end. The mere greatness of the World War has thwarted you; it has refused to become mere background, and obtrudes itself upon the stage as so much dead wood that will not burn with the dramatic fire. Dramatic action is a fire that must burn up everything but itself; there should be no room in a play for anything that does not belong to it, the whole history of the world must be reduced to wallpaper in front of which the characters must pose and speak.[6]

Theoretically Yeats's stand on what a play should contain was admirable. But in the context of O'Casey's plays and those of some others that were being produced at the Abbey, his dramatic conclusions seem odd. Besides, Yeats had over-reached himself in asserting that O'Casey was not interested in the Great War and was writing from his opinions. O'Casey was infuriated at Yeats's rejection of his play and wrote a letter challenging the poet's contentions with a series of questions:

You say—and this is the motif throughout the intonation of your whole song—that "I am not interested in the Great War." Now, how do you know that I am not interested in the Great War? Perhaps because I never mentioned it to you. Your statement is to me an impudently ignorant one to make, for it happens that I was and am passionately and intensely interested in the Great War. Throughout its duration I felt and talked of nothing else; brooded, wondered, and was amazed. . . . You say "you never stood on its battlefields." Do you really mean that no one should or could write about or speak about a war because one has not stood on the battlefields? Were you serious when you dictated that—really serious, now? Was Shakespeare at Actium or Philippi? Was G. B. Shaw in the boats with the French, or in the forts with the British when St. Joan and Dunois made the attack that relieved Orleans? And someone, I think, wrote a poem about Tir na nOg who never took a header into the land of Youth. And does war consist only of battlefields? [7]

Yeats made matters worse by suggesting in a letter to Lady Gregory (she forwarded this letter to O'Casey) that O'Casey could discreetly announce he had withdrawn the play "for revision" and thus save face. "There is going to be no damned secrecy with me surrounding the Abbey's rejection of the play," O'Casey thundered in his letter to Lennox Robinson and passed on the entire correspondence exchanged between him and the Abbey Directors to the London *Observer* and *The Irish Statesman*. So much for discretion.

Relations between O'Casey and the Abbey could have improved even at this stage when Lady Gregory got Yeats to agree to perform the play. But Lennox Robinson put his foot down: "No. It is a bad play." The last chance to bridge the rift between O'Casey and the Abbey was lost and they drifted apart. A year later, the Abbey started harassing O'Casey by not paying him his royalties when they were due and by trying to prevent Arthur Sinclair from producing *Juno and the Paycock* and *The Plough and the Stars* in Cork. All this further embittered O'Casey.

Peter Kavanagh writes that "the rejection of *The Silver Tassie* marked a weakening in the organizing faculty of Yeats's mind and a turning point in the Abbey Theatre's career as it moved down the hill to its ultimate collapse with the death of Yeats in 1939."[9] This is also the generally accepted view, but it is not altogether correct. No doubt Yeats was wrong in rejecting *The Silver Tassie*, even though he was convinced it was a bad play (a stand he maintained consistently till his death), for O'Casey by now had earned the right to get his plays produced and let the public judge for themselves. The point is that the Dublin public did get a chance to see this play seven years later and almost unanimously decried it. Of course, the reasons they gave were entirely different from those given by Yeats when he rejected it. Whether this play or O'Casey's subsequent plays, had he remained in cordial relation with the Abbey, could have saved the theatre is a matter for conjecture. From what we can see of the later plays, the answer is "No." The Abbey declined not because it lost O'Casey but because it lost the active participation and interest of its founder, W. B. Yeats.

Neither symbolism nor expressionism was totally absent in O'Casey's highly realistic Dublin plays. Of all the O'Casey commentators and critics, only Denis Johnston predicted with rare acumen the new technique at which the dramatist was groping. Writing in the pages of *The Living Age* as early as 1926, he said:

As for a new prophet, it is becoming increasing clear that as a realist, he [O'Casey] is an imposter. He will tell you the name and address of the person who made each individual speech in any of his plays, but we are not deceived by his protestations. His dialogue is becoming a series of word-poems in dialect, his plots are disappearing and giving place to a form of un-disguised Expressionism under the stress of a genius that is much too insistent and far too pregnant with meaning to be bound by the four dismal walls of ortho-dox realism. It will be interesting to see how long he will try to keep up so outrageous a pretense.[10]

In recent years, critics have shown great enthusiasm in pointing out the symbolism in O'Casey's early plays in an effort to relate them to his later works. Katharine Worth in her article "O'Casey's Dramatic Symbolism" and Vincent C. De Baun in "Sean O'Casey and the Road to Expressionism"[11] have with considerable insight shown the use of symbols in *Juno and the Paycock* and *The Plough and the Stars*, but both writers have gone to ex-tremes and in certain cases drawn conclusions which are untenable. Katherine Worth in her endeavour to find symbols and interpret them can go to the extent of saying: "The tenement house in *The Plough and the Stars* becomes so potent an image of Irish life that when the Tommies sit down to make tea in Bessie's room at the end of the play we know that we are watching the occu-pation of Ireland." This is not so; there is a lot of irony in this scene but no such symbolic meaning. To prove his thesis that in *The Plough and the Stars* O'Casey was well on the road to expressionism, Vincent De Baun can incorrectly profess that there is no "truly dominating personality" in this play, and add: "It is this 'levelness' of characterization which indicates a part of his first leaning towards expressionism." In these two criticisms one can see some of the hazards of symbolic interpretation.

In *The Shadow of a Gunman* the bag left by Maguire is a symbolic answer to Davoren's question: "And what danger can there be in being the shadow of a gunman?" In *Juno and the Paycock* the red votive light burning before the statue of the Virgin is symbolic; the house shorn of all its furniture towards the end of the play can be interpreted to stand for "a disintegrating family and a disintegrating country." In *The Plough and the Stars*, symbolism is even more predominant: one can trace it in some of the utterances of Bessie Burgess, in the silhouette of the Speaker and his fiery words in the second act, and in the introduction of the tri-colour. But not till we come to the second act of *The Silver Tassie* can we speak of expressionism with any great emphasis. The symbolism that we find in O'Casey's Dublin plays can be found in most naturalistic plays; even the most realistic scene or character is a symbol of something. As O'Casey put it: "even in the most commonplace of realistic plays the symbol can never be absent. A house on a stage can never be a house, and that which represents it must always be a symbol."[12]

O'Casey conceived *The Silver Tassie* while in Dublin, but wrote it after arriving in London. The title is taken from a song of Robert Burns, and the plot itself is based on the poem "Disabled" by Wilfred Owen. Reading the play one is immediately reminded of Wilfred Owen's fine sentence: "My subject is War, and the pity of War. The Poetry is in the pity."[13] The central figure is Harry Heegan, an athletic young man who goes to the trenches "as unthinkingly as he would go to the polling booth." He returns from the War an invalid to discover that the man who had carried him from the trenches has been awarded the Victoria Cross and has won the affection of the girl he loves. Through the agony of the crippled hero, O'Casey voices his trenchant hatred of war. In *Rose and Crown* he makes his purpose very clear:

> He would set down without malice or portly platitude the shattered enterprise of life to be endured by many of those who, not understanding the bloodied melody of war, went forth to fight, to die, or to return again with tarnished bodies and complaining minds. He would show a wide expanse of war in the midst of timorous hope and overweening fear; amidst a galaxy of guns; silently show the garlanded horror of war. . . . The ruin, the squeal of the mangled, the softening moan of the badly rended are horrible, be the battle just or unjust; be the fighters striving for the good or manifesting faith in evil.[14]

Many dramatists have condemned war by using the theme of a wounded body being derided by its surviving rivals, who are shown in health and strength. Somerset Maugham does it in *The Sacred Flame* and *For Services Rendered*, and Ernst Toller in *Hinkemann*. None of these plays, however, creates as strong an aversion for war as *The Silver Tassie*.

The opening act, in spite of all its realistic details, is as Shaw observed, "fantastic chanted poetry." Its chief purpose is to exalt Harry, and this is done by the two clowns, Sylvester and Simon, who recall his prowess. But the act is much too long for the material and full of cheap farce. Mrs Heegan's anxiety that her son may not miss the boat that is to take him to France rings false because of its exaggeration. When the gospel-preaching Susie tells her that desertion from active service means death, the mother exclaims: "An' my governmental money grant would stop at once."[15] What mother would say that? And O'Casey only four years ago had given us the greatest mother in drama—Juno! O'Casey's treatment of women in this play is far from flattering.

David Krause explaining this sudden change writes: "O'Casey here departs from his earlier sympathetic treatment of women because he is writing about an aspect of war which is not directly their tragedy, the holocaust of the battle-front.[16]" This explanation does not seem defensible: wherever sons, fathers, and husbands die, it is the women's tragedy. What O'Casey is trying to put forward, very much as Paul Raynal does in *The Unknown Warrior*, is that the people who stay at home cannot visualise what a grim thing war is.

The first act, like the rest of the play, is rich in religious symbols. Mr Winifred Smith in his fine study "The Dying God in the Modern Theatre" illumines some of these:

> . . . a second glance is more revealing, for it falls on the object in the middle of the room, a table covered with a purple cloth, like an altar, on which are displayed various gold and silver medals won by Harry; behind it a window opens towards the sea, showing a mast in the form of a cross, with a starry light at its top. Susie, quoting Scripture—an Old Testament prophecy of doom—as she polishes Harry's arms, is obviously the priestess serving the altar; just as obviously the two old men by the fire, in their reminiscences of the young hero's prowess, are the chorus celebrating the divine superiority of the chosen youth. These three prepare the entrance of Harry, who is at last borne into the room on the shoulders of a Bacchanalian crowd, the girls with "Their skirts kilted above their knees" in true Maenad fashion; he and his sweetheart, Jessie, drink from the Silver Tassie, the Grail, the cup of communion, that will soon be full of his blood as it is now full of the wine of rejoicing.[17]

O'Casey, though he came from a different faith, shows detailed knowledge of Roman Catholic rituals. When in his twenties he was strongly attracted towards Catholicism and, according to the Abbey Theatre Director Ernest Blythe, even carried rosary beads in his pocket.

Having established his characters in the first act, O'Casey in the second act moves on to show the horror and indecency of war. There were two ways in which he could do this: either in the naturalistic manner of *Journey's End*, where the effect of war is shown on a group of men huddled together under heavy bombardment, or by using expressionistic devices to gain breadth of effect and show war as the colossal nightmare it is. O'Casey wisely chose the latter method. The setting is a "jagged and lacerated ruin of what was once a monastery." There are no "banners," no "glittering spears," no "shouts of war." There is instead misery, pain, filth, and inertia. A broken crucifix leans forward, an arm released from the cross points towards the "white-faced" figure of the Virgin. Opposite the crucifix "is its living counterpart, a soldier with outstretched arms tied to a large wheel, enduring a penance for a minor infraction of army rules."[18] The characters have lost their identity; except for Barney and the Fourth Soldier described as very much like Teddy, none is recognisable. The proud Harry is now a nameless unit. Critics have puzzled as to why Harry is not shown in this act. There are two reasons for it: first, Harry can contribute nothing to a war that is impersonal. O'Casey sees nothing heroic in war, and wishes to emphasise that one who in civil life was an individual is in a war of such magnitude reduced to a number. The second reason is that O'Casey is keeping him away from all pain and hardship to show at an appropriate time how a man full of vitality and hope is suddenly reduced to a raging cripple. Barney is recognisable, for O'Casey wants to focus our attention on him. He is the one character who has not fused into the mass and is thus likely to escape the fate that befell his comrades-in-arm. Barney's stealing a cock belonging to a friendly state is symbolic of his later stealing his friend's girl.

The act opens with the Croucher dreamily intoning his prophecies of doom. These consist of parodies from the Book of Ezekiel, which roused strong protests in Dublin when the play was produced at the Abbey Theatre in August 1935. This is followed by the soldiers' chanting about their miserable lot, of bullets and shells and mud and vermin. Stretcher-bearers and the wounded sing their own song as they cross the stage on their way to the Red Cross Station; a pompous Visitor and a Staff Officer, "prim, pert, and polished" are introduced to heighten the irony through contrast. Finally the attack begins and all except Barney group round the howitzer to sing their litany:

CORPORAL [*singing*]:
> Hail, cool-hardened tower of steel emboss'd
> With the fever'd, figment thought of man;
> Gnardian [*sic*] of our love and hate and fear,
> Speak for us to the inner ear of God!

SOLDIERS:
> We believe in God and we believe in thee.[19]

There seems to be an echo here of Siegfried Sassoon's poem "The Kiss," which opens:

> To these I turn, in these I trust—
> Brother Lead and Sister Steel.
> To his blind power I make appeal,
> I guard her beauty clean from rust.[20]

Much of the poetry is not of the first order and the act's chief appeal lies in O'Casey's stage technique and presentation. More than one critic who was disappointed on reading the play was converted in its favour on seeing it performed at the Apollo Theatre, London, in October 1929.

Shaw has described the last two acts as full of the "fiercest ironic realism."[21] They have an abundance of realistic details but are not realistic in the sense in which

O'Casey's early works are. The third act is not necessary to the action of the play. O'Casey should in fact have moved straight from the expressionistic second act to the fourth act. As it stands, it exposes the conclusion prematurely and weakens O'Casey's purpose of creating revulsion against war. Still, how beautiful and carefully worked out the third act is. It opens with Sylvester and Simon, who are in hospital for trifling ailments. Gradually Harry, who has been paralysed from the waist down, is introduced: he twice silently wheels himself in and out on an invalid chair. His terrible plight is brought into contrast with the serio-comic attitude of Sylvester and Simon. Little by little he speaks, and with each word he utters the tragedy is built up as if "by bricks and mortar." The climax comes with Harry's cry of despair— "God of the miracles, give a poor devil a chance, give a poor devil a chance"—tossed against the passionless Latin chanting of the nuns to the Virgin Mother:

> Salve Regina, mater misericordiae;
> Vitae dulcedo et spes nostra, salve![22]

The bitter irony, as Hogan points out, "is certainly one of O'Casey's finest touches."[23]

The time for miracles is over. The final act is set in the Avondale Football Club—the scene of the crippled Harry's former triumph. Those who have returned sound in body and mind from the trenches make merry: the ascetic Susie has found her man in the heartless surgeon Maxwell and the fickle Jessie hers in the once loyal Barney, who carried Harry to safety from the line of fire. As the two pairs dance and twirl in joy, Harry, tormented by his love for Jessie, speaks what must be one of the most painful utterances in any play:

To the dancing, for the day cometh when no man can play. And legs were made to dance, to run, to jump, to carry you from one place to another; but mine can

neither walk, nor run, nor jump, nor feel the merry
motion of a dance. But stretch me on the floor fair on
my belly, and I will turn over on my back, then
wriggle back again on to my belly; and that's more
than a dead, dead man can do![24]

This poignant utterance is juxtaposed with the comicality
of Sylvester and Simon, as they answer the telephone:

SIMON: If you want me to work the thing properly,
you'll have to keep yourself from interfering. [*Resum-
ing surlily*] Eh, hallo, listen, yes? Ha! ha! ha! ha! Yes,
yes, yes. No, no, no. Cheerio! Yes. Eh, hallo, listen,
eh. Hallo.
SYLVESTER: What is it? What're they sayin'?
SIMON [*hopelessly, taking the receiver from his ear*]:I don't
seem to be able to hear a damn sound.
SYLVESTER: An' Holy God, what are you yessin' and
noin' and cheerioin' out of you for then?
SIMON: You couldn't stand here like a fool and say
nothing, could you?[25]

This may be music-hall stuff, but as Nathan somewhere
says: "superb music-hall remains nonetheless still
superb."

The orgy increases and with it the despair of Harry
and Teddy (the latter has been blinded in the War)
Sylvester rightly remarks: "What's a decoration to an
hospital is an anxiety here";[26] and behind the callous
admonishment of Susie there is a firm truth:

Oh nonsense! If you'd passed as many through your
hands as I, you'd hardly notice one. [*To Jessie*]
Jessie, Teddy Foran and Harry Heegan have gone to
live their own way in another world. Neither I nor you
can lift them out of it. No longer can they do the
things we do. We can't give sight to the blind or make
the lame walk. We would if we could. It is the mis-
fortune of war. As long as wars are waged, we shall be

vexed by woe; strong legs shall be made useless and bright eyes made dark. But we, who have come through the fire unharmed, must go on living.[27]

In the opening paragraph of *Lady Chatterley's Lover* D. H. Lawrence says, "We've got to live, no matter how many skies have fallen." O'Casey through Susie reiterates this. For Harry and Teddy there is darkness, which in the latter's words "stretches from the throne of God to the end of the hearth of hell."[28] No individual, but the institution of war is responsible for their plight. The obvious message of the play is that war must be banished from the earth at all cost. This may be propaganda, but there is truth in it we are willing to endorse to-day.

Harry and Teddy depart and the dance resumes; Surgeon Maxwell sings as the curtains come down:

> For he is a life on the ebb,
> We a full life on the flow![29]

Two critics have shown fine perception in their interpretation of the conclusion of the play. Winifred Smith writes: "O'Casey, like Werfel, though less romantically, has expressed the feelings of many of his generation, that the cosmic rhythm of destruction and creation is not only eternal but essentially amoral."[30] And Wilson Knight says: "O'Casey's uncompromising belief in the right to happiness for those who can find it resists even his sense of suffering in those who cannot. This is high dramatic thinking."[31]

Wilson Knight has made a notable point. On the surface this song is an ironic comment on the situation, the irony being very similar to what we saw in *Juno and the Paycock* and *The Plough and the Stars*. But deep down and on a more significant level it is O'Casey's first affirmation to life: that one must expel sorrow and embrace joy and happiness. His Dublin plays were marked by cynicism, bitterness, and the horrible impact of poverty; the plays he wrote in England have as their

underlying theme the quest for joy. He lambasts every
institution, political or religious, that stands between
man and his right to happiness.

Having exploited the possibilities of symbolic drama
in the second act of *The Silver Tassie*, O'Casey set out
to write a completely expressionistic play, *Within the
Gates*. *The Silver Tassie* was a transitional play: no longer
were all the scenes set in Dublin; no strong emphasis
was laid on depicting slum life, and war that had been
a background became the leading *motif*. In technique
the departure was even greater. Colours, symbols, songs,
stylisation of speech and rhythmic patterns were introduced. A cosmic concern began to govern his works
and expressionism seemed a better medium of com-
munication with the audience. Naturalism was relegated
to the background and used only in the service of
expressionism. The juxtaposition of tragedy and comedy
(the very hall-mark of his success) yielded precedence
to the juxtaposition of symbolism and realism; not only
were acts written in different manners mixed with one
another but so were even small scenes and incidents.
O'Casey's strong attack on naturalism when offering
Within the Gates to the public in London and New York
in 1934—

I am out to destroy the accepted naturalistic presentation of character; to get back to the poetic significance of drama.[32]
. . . all fresh and imaginatively minded dramatists
are out to release drama from the pillory of naturalism
and send her dancing through the streets. . . .[33]

—is not without its irony, for some of the best scenes in
the play, such as the soap-box speakers arguing on
"spice-time," are in the naturalistic rather than the
symbolic vein.

O'Casey's visits to Hyde Park, London, suggested a
theme to him and brought him in touch with characters

whose potentialities had never been explored. He had first thought of doing a film script, for the cinema would have been better able to capture the varied life he wished to portray. But O'Casey's poor opinion of films and Hitchcock's reluctance to pursue the matter settled the question: O'Casey writes:

> He had written a lot of dialogue and rough drafts of themes, and now he was trying to knit the wild themes and wandering dialogue into a design of Morning, Noon, Evening, and Night, blending these in with the seasons, changing the outlook of the scenes by changing the colour of flower and tree, blending these again with the moods of the scenes. The dominant colour of Morning and Spring was to be a light, sparkling green, that of Noon crimson and gold; Autumn's crimson was to tinge itself with violet, and Winter and Night were to be violet, turning to purple, and black.[34]

The four scenes (each scene constitutes an act) are set at a time of day appropriate to the season concerned, thus playing on diurnal rhythms also. There is a metaphysic within this studied patterning. Close significances are implicit in chosen moments of bird-song and sunshine; human action in all instances is related to seasonal references. Colours on the stage abound and the play is full of colourful words (a heritage from Celtic literature). The dialogue, not always brilliant, is stylised, and the entry and exit of the numerous characters and their positions on the stage are expertly controlled. Music and dance are closely woven into the symbolic pattern of the drama; they do not merely further the theme but contain it as well. The play is a triumph of technique and stage-craft.

It is not easy to give a summary of the plot. It is multi-directional: themes social, religious, sexual, political, scientific interlace the pattern. At the barest it is a picture of contemporary London; in its wider symbolic significance, a picture of society as we have constituted it. How complex and wide is the subject treated can be judged from some of the epithets used to sum up the play. It has been called a "microcosm of modern civilisation," a "microcosm of human life," a "dramatization of the Waste-land of the post-war world," an "allegory of the modern world," and a "twentieth-century morality play." The impressions it has left on critics vary greatly. James Agate dismissed it as "pretentious rubbish" and Joseph Wood Krutch as "Mr. O'Casey's Charade." On the other hand, Wilson Knight calls it "O'Casey's most comprehensive achievement," and Nathan wrote that it is "one of the finest plays of our time." If these opinions serve any purpose it is to encourage every reader to formulate his own impressions without any sense of embarrassment.

The three principal characters are the Bishop, the Dreamer, and the Young Woman. The Young Woman, who is the illegitimate daughter of the Bishop, has been forced by circumstances to become a prostitute. She is torn by conflicting emotions: on the one hand she wishes to live a life of joy, sex, and unrestrained youth, on the other hand she seeks the salvation which her present mode of life denies her. The Bishop and the Dreamer, holding views that are diametrically opposite, struggle to win the Young Woman over to their beliefs. The Dreamer's approach to God is through song and dance; the Bishop's through prayer and repentance. In the beginning it seems a hard choice for the Young Woman, but as the play progresses the dramatist indicates that the gulf between the Dreamer's point of view and that of the Bishop is not as wide as official religion would suggest. The Young Woman dies dancing and the Bishop prays: "O Lord, who taketh pleasure in Thy people, let this dance be unto Thee as a merry prayer offered by an innocent and excited child!"[35]

The Bishop's concession no doubt suggests a victory for the Dreamer, but it at the same time suggests a victory of the Bishop over himself. The end also suggests that it was not the Young Woman who had become un-Christian, but Christianity that had cut itself off from Christ. The Church triumphs in accepting the unrepentant, yet trusting, whore.

The play has been strongly attacked for being anti-moral and anti-Christian. Quite a few critics took exception to the Bishop's being shown as the father of the young prostitute. James Agate, who had hailed O'Casey's earlier plays as the greatest in the theatre since the days of the Elizabethans, wrote: "Mr. Douglas Jefferies had a fair shot at the Bishop, though Mr. O'Casey obviously contemplated an oilier scoundrel."[36] And the critic Desmond MacCarthy wrote: "What heavy and artificially loaded irony to make 'The Bishop' the father of 'The Prostitute'! How cheap!"[37] When the play was on its American tour in 1934, the clergy in Boston protested so strongly that its showing was banned. No doubt there is an anti-clerical note in it, but the play is not irreligious, nor is the Bishop a scoundrel.

The opinions quoted above are all based on the 1934 version of the play. In the revised version (the one I am discussing here) the Bishop has been a little more generously portrayed, but the change is not so great as to make the criticism against the Bishop based on the first version invalid. O'Casey made him the father of the Young Woman for two very specific reasons. Through the Bishop he attacks the concept of celibacy. Not only does the practice of celibacy bar the clergy from a sympathetic understanding of sexual problems but it also leads to sexual irregularities, as was indicated in Brian Merriman's, "The Midnight Court," possibly the greatest of Irish satiric poems. Showing the Bishop as the father of the Young Woman also helps to make him a person of dramatic interest, and in this play which

has at least twenty characters (the 1934 version that
was played in London and New York had twenty-seven)
the Bishop is the only one that develops sufficiently. His
tragedy is both spiritual and human, and the situation
he faces is a most complex one. Short of admitting that
he is her father (a step that would be more courageous
than wise), he does everything possible to help his
daughter. He gives her the little money he has, he runs
considerable risk to save her; and he suffers himself to
be insulted by her and by the other Park visitors.

No doubt there are moments when the Bishop has no
satisfactory answer to the questions posed by the Young
Woman and others. His inadequacy takes the form of
embarrassment: and on the whole the serious omissions
in our religious consciousness are just such as would not
necessarily offend, but rather embarrass. The Bishop is
embarrassed quite often: not least at the Young Woman's
response to his anxiety for caution while helping her:

BISHOP [*rather sternly*]: Listen, child, then, and be
serious. When trying to help you, I must be careful
of what others may think.
YOUNG WOMAN: Why have you to be careful? Can't
you yourself pray, or push yourself out of the fear of
what may be said about you? What does it matter how
many say a man's a sinner if God thinks him a saint?[38]

That the Bishop has no answer to this is not the short-
coming of Christianity, but of its priests. That the
Bishop should later endorse the Young Woman's
persuasion is greatly to his credit:

BISHOP'S SISTER: If you go on like this much longer,
Gilbert, you'll find yourself becoming ridiculous to
respectable and important opinion.
BISHOP [*vehemently*]: That has been my besetting sin
all along—fear of the respectable opinion of others. I
renounce it now! She herself has said, What does it
matter how many think a man to be a sinner if God

believes him to be a saint. That's what she said—to my very face.[39]

The Dreamer is O'Casey's chief spokesman. The leaflet that was inserted in the programme when the play was shown at the National Theatre, New York, included, in addition to O'Casey's views on expressionism, an account of what the various characters symbolise. O'Casey described the Dreamer as:

. . . symbol of a noble restlessness and discontent; of the stir in life that brings to birth new things and greater things than those that were before; of the power realizing that the urge of life is above the level of conventional morality; of ruthlessness to get near to the things that matter, and sanctify them with intelligence, energy, gracefulness and song; of rebellion against stupidity; and of the rising intelligence in man that will no longer stand, nor venerate, nor shelter those whom poverty of spirit has emptied of all that is worth while in life.[40]

All this is a very noble utterance, however abstruse, but it piles together more than a symbol can hold. In addition to the description of the Dreamer, O'Casey gave descriptions of sixteen other characters, many of them phrased equally vaguely. This gave the critics an excellent stick to beat the play with. The *Daily Worker* commented that the dramatist found it necessary "to confess his brainchild a cripple by sending it out propped on both sides on crutches of theory."[41] Ward Williamson rightly says that the prudent course would have been to let the play establish these facts rather than insist upon them in print.[42] But then when has O'Casey ever been prudent in his dealings with producers, critics, and public?

I find on re-reading the play that the Dreamer disappoints. He does not do a day's honest work but saunters about the Park cursing the kill-joys in a most violent and unbecoming manner and pleading for a

vigorous life in the language of a priggish undergraduate.
Here are some of his words to the two chair attendants:

Here, you two derelict worshippers of fine raiment—
when are you going to die?[43]

Away, and cower in your corner, till life hoodooes you
out of the misery you both love! Away, the pair of
you, you make a nightmare of the dream of God![44]

Kill off the withered mind, the violently-stupid, O
Lord, who have nothing to give, have nothing to get![45]

He calls the Bishop a "purple-button'd deadman," a
most unjust remark; he uses the money the Bishop had
given him for the Young Woman to entice her; he
advises her to "transmute vague years of life into a
glowing hour of love" for reasons that suit his plan. His
concern for the Young Woman is a little too intricately
interwoven with concern for himself. If he still manages
to succeed on the stage, it is partly because except for
the Bishop and the Young Woman he has no rivals, and
also because he voices the noble admonition to approach
life and death with a song and a dance. This may be
a platitude, but it surely needs to be reaffirmed in
sick times such as ours. O'Casey's plays are a protest
against the pessimism of Toller, Brecht, Capek, Elmer
Rice, O'Neill, and others.

The Young Woman has her origin in Nannie, the
principal character in O'Casey's one-act play called
Nannie's Night Out. This play was performed at the
Abbey Theatre in October 1924 and is included in
Feathers from the Green Crow. O'Casey has described the
Young Woman as a "symbol of those young women full
of life and a fine energy, gracious and kind, to whom
life fails to respond, and who are determined to be
wicked rather than virtuous out of conformity or fear."[46]
The Young Woman is nowhere shown determined to be
wicked. She has a great zest for life, and like most young

women she seeks security and motherhood. It is here
that life has failed to respond to her. O'Casey used her
as a sensitive instrument to weigh the Bishop's point of
view against that of the Dreamer, and though throughout
the play she tilts the scales a little to the side of the
Dreamer, in the end the pans are balanced.

Underlying the serious theme, there is plenty of
comedy. Nobody who has spent a Sunday afternoon in
Hyde Park can fail to see O'Casey's unique genius in
capturing his people as they are in real life. Here is a
scene worth quoting at length:

MAN WITH UMBRELLA: Now we all know that the
clock created time, en' the measuring-rod created
spice, so that there is really neither spice nor time;
but there is such a thing as spice-time. See? Get that?
MAN WEARING TRILBY [*with confidence*]: Quite; that
much is perfectly clear.
MAN WITH UMBRELLA: Right. Now, suppose that one
night, when we all slept, th' universe we knows sank
down to the size of a football, en' all the clocks began
to move a thousand times quicker,—no, slower—it
wouldn't mike the slightest difference to us, for we
wouldn't realize that any difference 'ad tyken plice,
though each of us would live a thousand times longer,
en' man couldn't be seen, even under a microscope.
GUARDSMAN [*jocularly*]: Could a woman be seen under
a microscope?
MAN WEARING CAP [*to Guardsman*]: Levity's outa
plice, friend, when men are trying to think out th'
truth of things.
GUARDSMAN: But 'ow could th' world sink dahn to
th' size of a football? Doesn't seem a sife thing to me.
MAN WITH UMBRELLA [*with cold dignity*]: I said *if* it
did, friend.
GUARDSMAN [*trying to find a way out*]: Yes; but if a man
couldn't be seen under a microscope, wot abaht 'is kids?

MAN WITH UMBRELLA: I simply styted a hypothenuse, friend.

MAN WEARING CAP [to Guardsman]: It's only en hypothenuse, you understand? [To Man with Umbrella] But it's en impossible one, I think. D'ye mean that under your hypothenuse, en hour of the clock would stretch aht into ten years of time?

MAN WITH UMBRELLA: Exactly that is spice-time; en 'undred years if you like.

MAN WEARING CAP: Wot? Then in your spice-time, a man doin' eight hours would be workin' for eight 'undred years!

GUARDSMAN [to Man with Umbrella]: You're barmy, man! Wot abaht th' bloke doin' penal servitide fer life? When is 'e agoin' to get aht? You're barmy, man!

NURSEMAID [to Guardsman—chucking his arm]: Are you comin', Harry? If you don't 'urry, I'll 'ave to go, en' you'll 'ave to go withaht even a firewell squeeze.

MAN WITH UMBRELLA [annoyed—to Guardsman]: Look, friend, if I was you, I'd go with the girl; for it's pline your mind 'asn't been educyted yet to grasp the complicyted functions of wot we know as spice-time problems.

GUARDSMAN [with heat]: 'Oo 'asn't a mind? 'Oo're you to sye I 'asn't a mind? I 'asn't a mind as would warn't to tern th' world into a football. It's a punch on the jawr you warnts for thinkin' people warnts the world to be a football. Wye's there different thoughts in every mind, en' different rules in every country? Becorse people like you 'as th' world turned upside dahn! Wot do I mean when I syes th' world is upside dahn? Why, I means th' whole world is upside dahn, en' ennyone as 'as a mind'll unnerstend me![47]

Here then is O'Casey of the Dublin plays with none of his powers in decline. If the play is a lesser work than *The Plough and the Stars* it is because it lacks intensity: an intensity that was supplied in his earlier plays by his great love for Ireland and his passionate involvement in the struggle for Irish freedom. O'Casey is not an intellectual artist as Shaw was; he is a man of "emotion" and the "heart." And Ireland most supplied his emotional needs.

Within the Gates is O'Casey's most Christian play. In its patterning it follows the Breviary and the Missal; the Spring and Summer choruses are a variation on the psalms of the morning hours, Matins and Lauds; Biblical phraseology abounds and many passages from the Bible are parodied to convey the anguish of the characters. Brooks Atkinson, angered by the way the Boston clergymen behaved, rightly said: "God is his [O'Casey's] greatest character."[48] The play nowhere attacks religion, but it does attack a Church that through the ages has drifted away from Christ and to-day thrives by keeping the picture of hell fire before us. The Saviour should be loved, not feared. And what greater love can we show Him, asks O'Casey, than that we rejoice in His world and come in His presence with a song and a dance? O'Casey also takes the clergy to task for being suspicious of sexual love and for failing to relate Christianity to sexual urges. Furthermore, he assails the killjoys symbolised by the Chair Attendants, the Evangelists, the Salvationists, and the Down-and-Outs. When he makes one of his Chair Attendants say, "Mide me feel prahd to be en Englishman!" he is clearly sneering at the chauvinism in Noel Coward's *Cavalcade* and the author's curtain speech: ". . . it is still a pretty exciting thing to be English." O'Casey, the Irishman, does not think so, and he makes this even more clear in *Purple Dust*.

REFERENCES

1. H. Shipp, "The Art of Sean O'Casey," *The English Review*, 42, Jun. 1926, p. 852.
2. E.S.A., "Mr. O'Casey Again," *The Spectator*, 136, 29 May 1926, p. 904.
3. Letter to me from O'Casey dated 20 Apr. 1958.
4. *G.C.*, p. 165.
5. *Punch*, 9 Mar. 1955.
6. *The Irish Statesman*, 10, 9 Jun. 1928, p. 269.

7. *Op. cit.*, p. 271.

8. *Op. cit.*, p. 269.

9. *The Story of the Abbey Theatre*, 1950, p. 143.

10. "Sean O'Casey: An Appreciation," 329, 17 Apr. 1926, p. 163.

11. Both articles are included in *Modern Drama*, 4, Dec. 1961.

12. *G.C.*, p. 83.

13. *Poems*, ed. Edmund Blunden, 1920, p. 40.

14. *Rose and Crown*, pp. 29-30.

15. *S.T.*, p. 18.

16. Krause, p. 113.

17. *Review of Religion*, 5, Mar. 1941, pp. 270-1.

18. *Op. cit.*, p. 271.

19. *S.T.*, p. 54.

20. *Collected Poems 1908-1956*, 1961, p. 15.

21. Quoted in *Lady Gregory's Journals*, 1946, p. 111.

22. *S.T.*, p. 78.

23. Hogan, p. 68.

24. *S.T.*, p. 82.

25. *S.T.*, pp. 86-7.

26. *S.T.*, p. 83.

27. *S.T.*, p. 103.

28. *S.T.*, p. 89.

29. *S.T.*, p. 103.

30. *Review of Religion*, 5, Mar. 1941, pp. 272-3.

31. *The Golden Labyrinth*, 1962, p. 376. Mr Knight's eight pages are the best piece of that length on the dramatist.

32. *The New York Times*, 26 Mar. 1934.

33. *Sunday Times*, 21 Oct. 1934.

34. *Rose and Crown*, pp. 152-3.

35. *W.G.*, p. 229.

36. *The Flying Wasp*, p. 48.

37. *Drama*, 1940, p. 350.

38. *W.G.*, p. 191.

39. *W.G.*, p. 205.

40. Quoted in Cowasjee, p. 145.

41. Leon Alexander, "Sean O'Casey Tilts a Dull Lance Against Puritanism in Play 'Within the Gates'," *Daily Worker*, 27 Oct. 1934,

42. Ward Williamson, *An Analytical History of American Criticism of the Works of Sean O'Casey, 1924-1958*, 1962. This is an excellent unpublished Ph.D. dissertation in the library of the State University of Iowa.

43. *W.G.*, p. 120.

44. *W.G.*, p. 122.

45. *W.G.*, p. 132.

46. Quoted in Jules Koslow's *The Green and the Red*, 1949, p. 70.

47. *W.G.*, pp. 209-10.

48. *The New York Times*, 23 Oct. 1934.

CHAPTER IV

O'CASEY AND COMMUNISM

For our purpose, O'Casey's remaining plays may conveniently be divided into two groups: (1) plays concerned primarily with Communism; (2) plays expressing O'Casey's views on life in Ireland. Technique, characterisation, humour, and a strong urge to promote happiness for all are common to these two groups. Though I am dividing the plays on the basis of content, they should not be judged on their content alone but all factors that constitute good drama should be taken into consideration. A play is not bad because it propagates a faith, but only if in doing so it loses some of its dramatic qualities. O'Casey's hard lot was that much of his work was dismissed on the basis of content (his espousal of Communism and his assault on organised religion) and little attention was paid to the splendour of his language, his often rich characterisation, expert stage-craft, and much else. Still, content is important to a play and it was not for nothing that Aristotle declared the plot to be the soul of the drama. Very often a weak plot leads to weak characterisation, dialogue, and setting.

A little should be said about O'Casey's peculiar brand of Communism—one that at times embarrassed his comrades as much as it intrigued his non-Communist friends. O'Casey repeatedly said that he was a born Communist. If he was a Communist from the very beginning, then how was it that he, who had revealed so much of himself and his beliefs in his early books, did not portray the Socialists sympathetically till he was sixty years of age? Why were Jimmy and the Covey ridiculed respectively in *Juno and the Paycock* and *The Plough and the Stars*? Why did the leftist *Daily Worker* come down so heavily on *The Plough and the Stars* and *Within the Gates*? To add to the confusion, we now have O'Casey's early articles published in *Feathers from the Green Crow*, in some of which he does not speak like a Socialist at all. In an article published in *The Irish Worker* of 22 Feb. 1913 and called " 'Euchan' and Ireland, a Challenge to a Verbal Combat," O'Casey writes:

The delivery of Ireland is not in the Labour Manifesto, good and salutary as it may be, but in the strength, beauty, nobility and imagination of the Gaelic ideal.[1]

And a few days later he wrote in *Irish Freedom*:

But woe unto us if we hand over our ideals to be squared and shaped and glossed by those who would write in our skies that socialism is Ireland's hope, and hang around our necks the green ribbons of 'Cumannacht ne hEireann.'[2]

My own feeling is that O'Casey when a Dublin working man had no definite opinion on Socialism and was not sure if it was the answer to the world's problems. His main concern was Ireland and the welfare of the Irish working class. In a country still fighting for freedom, one could not put down the plight of the workers merely to capitalistic exploitation; there was the question of foreign domination first and foremost. It was only after O'Casey came to London and witnessed the Great Depression of the early 1930s that his views became firmly defined. He found that political emancipation was worth little if it could not root out hunger, unemployment, and starvation. He saw that the problems the workers faced were not peculiar to Ireland but similar to those they faced all over the world. The workers of the world must unite and fight for their rights. The slogan captured his imagination and Moscow became his Mecca. He was saluting the Soviet Socialistic Revolution for many years prior to his death in September 1964, and neither the 1956 revolt in Hungary nor anything else ever disillusioned him.

When O'Casey said he was a born Communist, he meant no more than that he was always concerned for the welfare of the poor and the down-trodden. The hunger and privation he suffered and saw his fellow-men suffer left a deep impression on him, and it was greatly to his credit that the change in his personal fortune in no way affected his convictions. His affiliation to the Communist party was a much later occurrence, having much to do with his notion that Christianity had failed. A highly religious man, he was grieved to see the Church sit idle in the midst of oppression and injustice. The need of a faith and his immense humanity drove him to embrace Communism openly. John Macmurray accurately observes:

Christianity is the source of Communism, and Communism has moved into dialectical opposition to Christianity through the process by which Christianity in its conscious form has been divorced from material realities.[3]

In theory, there is a striking similarity between Communism and the New Testament: a fact that fitted in wonderfully with O'Casey's mental make-up. But in practice one finds that Communism is as divorced from its principles as Christianity is from its. This enigma O'Casey solved by an act of faith: by believing that in course of time and after the necessary bloodshed and horror Communism would bring everlasting peace and happiness to mankind.

A few things should be borne in mind when speaking of O'Casey's Communism. First, it consists not in reaction against Christianity but in reaction against what a *bourgeois* Christian society preaches but does not practise.

Its purpose is to fulfill Christ's prophecy: that the hungry shall be filled with good things. Second, it is not manifested as a Marxist invention, but as a social growth that has developed through the ages, since men came together to protect themselves from the "mammoth and tiger of the sabre-tooth." The disassociation of Communism from Marxism was very much to O'Casey's purpose, for Marxists do not believe in God while God was fundamental to O'Casey's thinking. This, of course, created problems: the Communists felt that he was unnecessarily re-creating the God they had killed, while the Christians objected to Christ's being clad in red. Both were wrong, for as O'Casey saw it Communism is Christ's kingdom on earth. Communism is not replacing Christ, it is replacing a Church that has failed Christ. O'Casey had nothing against heaven, all he wanted was that the poor should have a share of this earth as well.

The Star Turns Red (1940) is on the whole disappointing work and one the dramatist never risked defending against the onslaught of critics. It is dedicated to the men and women who fought through the Dublin Lock-Out in 1913; the time of the setting is "To-morrow or the next day." Though the locale is not stated, one can see from the characterisation (the Lord Mayor is a caricature of a well-known past Lord Mayor of Dublin; Red Jim is drawn from Jim Larkin) and the influence the Church wields in social and political matters that it is Dublin. The plot centres upon the battle between the Communists and the Fascists, which, of course, the Communists win. The play opens with the two brothers, Jack (Communist) and Kain (Fascist), confronting each other. Michael, the father of Jack's sweetheart, Julia, enters and asks Jack to persuade her not to go to the dance but to come to the Union Hall instead. There is a raid by the Fascist storm-troopers who are accompanied by the Purple Priest of the Christian Front. There is an exchange of abuses between the two opposing groups, and Julia then slaps the Fascist leader. She is taken out to be whipped, when her father arrives and is shot by Kain while trying to rescue her. Comrade Michael dies with a clenched fist salute after entrusting the Cause and Julia to Jack's care. Meanwhile the Union leaders at the instigation of the Purple Priest make a futile attempt to dislodge their leader Red Jim and sabotage the strike. The Brown Priest, who sympathises with the workers, informs Red Jim about the imminent attack against them by the Saffron Shirts (Fascists) and the police. The inevitable battle takes place, but not before there has been a long struggle between the Communists and the Purple Priest to claim the body of Michael. In the fight Jack is killed, but O'Casey indicates that the Communists are in fact victorious. The play ends with Jim comforting the weeping Julia: "He's not too far away to hear what's happening. You'll nurse, now, a far greater thing than a darling dead man. Up, young woman, and join in the glowing hour your lover died to fashion. He fought for life, for life is all; and death is nothing!"[4]

The play has been severely criticised, even by O'Casey's most ardent admirers. David Krause, who has written movingly about O'Casey under chapter titles such as "Prometheus of Dublin" and "The Playwright as Prophet," says:

Even if one makes allowances for the fact that rampart [sic] Fascism was at the height of its power when O'Casey wrote this play, it is difficult to accept it as either successful propaganda or drama. There are times when the play threatens to assume the epic violence of Picasso's 'Guernica', but too often O'Casey's moral outrage is spent in sentimental invective and as a result the play seldom rises about the level of a proletarian thriller.[5]

And Robert Hogan, who tells me that he has modified

some of the opinions he expressed in *The Experiments of Sean O'Casey*, writes there:

> *The Star* is the closest to straight propaganda that O'Casey has written, and it is his poorest play. . . . There is no real dramatic clash here because there are no characters. There is only disembodied opinion. Presumably the play taught O'Casey the difficulties of proceeding so far into didacticism, for never again does he stray so far from character.[6]

James Agate, the critic O'Casey has most attacked in *The Flying Wasp* (1937), surprised everybody by calling the play "a masterpiece" in the *Sunday Times* of 17 Mar. 1940. In saying so he only lived up to what O'Casey said of him: "This was the fatal flaw in Agate's criticism —he couldn't tell a miserable play from a great one."[7]

The play falls short of O'Casey's greatness not because it advocates Communism but because it lacks dramatic fire. The characters are divided into two groups: the Communists, who have all the virtues in the world, and the Fascists and their followers, who are the very embodiment of evil. The result is that there is no dramatic conflict within the minds of the characters, except for a little in the Brown Priest and in Kain. The *dramatis personae* are used only to expound a morality, or as Walter Kerr puts it: "the people are digits, adding up to the correct ideological sum."[8]

O'Casey does this intentionally; he is writing a proletarian drama in which message is far more important than artistry. Any conflict in the minds of the characters might create conflict in the minds of the audience, and so he keeps good separate from evil. This explains the numerous characters in the play. To take one instance, he had to introduce the Brown Priest in contrast to the Purple Priest, to emphasise that all priests are not wicked. In *Within the Gates* one priest sufficed, for O'Casey could safely show the good and the evil in the same person.

and let the good triumph over the evil. But such a course could not be followed in a play which in essence was straight propaganda, for nothing is more fatal to propaganda than conflict or doubt. In *The Star Turns Red* O'Casey has done all the thinking for his comrades and given them the solution.

The abundance of invective and epithets indiscriminately hurled at each other by the Communists and Fascists detracts much from the drama. Here are just a few of them: "litany-lit bowsy," "hopabout little bugger," "slug-soul'd renegade," "envy-stippled titivated toads," "shiny-coloured dressing gown," "golden-snouted snails," "you shattered idea of a man made backwards," "you tattered tail-end of a false beginning," "you pale hypothesis of a needless life," "under-sized cut," "sly circumstance of life," "oozy scum." Much of the language is unnecessarily violent and hysterical, and in Act IV the stage is virtually strewn with corpses: "each with a stiffened clenched fist held high." All this stands in sharp contrast to the pacifism of the early plays and O'Casey's trenchant denunciation of war. No doubt the dramatist has changed his mind in favour of a militant attitude and is prepared to accept bloodshed for a political end. Not entirely political, for O'Casey may well say that it is for a religious and social cause: a few must die so that the millions may live.

Except for the love between mother and child, family ties have no place in O'Casey's plays. This is possibly the result of his own unhappy childhood: his father died when he was a child and his brothers and sisters gave him little love. In this play family ties have no meaning whatsoever.

OLD WOMAN: Jack, Jack, he is your brother.

JACK: I have brothers everywhere, Mother; but I have none in this house.

OLD WOMAN: He is my son; you are my son: therefore you are his brother.

F

JACK: He is dead; I see him not, I hear him not, I touch
him not—he is dead.[9]

These sentiments may please comrades who put the
Cause above life and political affiliations above blood
ties. But there is also much in the play that might dis-
turb them. The behaviour of the drunkard Brannigan—
for whom "a hold-up is Communism in practice"—and
the corruption of the Union leaders brings little credit
to the Workers' Movement. Nor can O'Casey's attempt
to bring the acquiescence of Christianity to the revolutionary triumph of the Communists be altogether wel-
come to the comrades. It is interesting that O'Casey's
most popular work in Russia is *Juno and the Paycock* and
the first two volumes of his autobiographies, not *The
Star Turns Red* and the last two volumes of his autobiographies in which he sings of Communism and
showers his blessings on the Great Socialistic Revolution.

The most significant feature of the play is O'Casey's
endeavour to relate Christianity to Communism. More
than any other work of his, this is saturated with Christian
ideas, imagery, and Biblical language. The action takes
place on a Christmas Eve and is presumably over before
Christmas Day dawns; the silver star is the Star of
Bethlehem (it shines near the church steeple in the first
three acts, but moves close to the foundry chimney in
the last act and turns red to signify the triumph of the
workers). The second act is set in the General Workers'
Union and the stage directions tell us that there is "a
white cross on which a red hammer and sickle are
imposed." Red Jim begs the Brown Priest to stay with
them: "To be with us when the star turns red; to help
us to carry the fiery cross."[10] A true priest of God should
be present, for the occasion is a highly religious one for
O'Casey: the workers have united to fulfill Christ's
prophecy.

Communism and Christianity are further woven together through dialogue. The more intensely Communist

a character is, the more strongly he believes in God. In the world of the traitors such as Brallain, Caheer, Sheasker, Eglish, God has no place, but plays a large part in the lives of Red Jim, Jack, and Julia. But their God is not the God portrayed by the corrupt Churches, but the God those Churches have betrayed. Here is a characteristic utterance from Red Jim:

> If the heritage of heaven be the heritage here of shame and rags and the dead puzzle of poverty, then we turn our backs on it! If your God stands for one child to be born in a hovel and another in a palace, then we declare against him. If your God declares that one child shall be clad in silks and another in sores, then we declare against him. If your God declares that it takes a sack of sovereigns to keep one child and a handful of pence to keep another, then we declare against him. If your God declares that one child shall dwell in the glory of knowledge and another shall die in the poverty of ignorance, then we declare against him: once and for all and for ever we declare against your God, who hath filled the wealthy with good things and hath sent the poor empty away.[11]

In bringing Communism and Christianity so close that the two seem one (the dramatist even denies that there is Communist dogma in the play—he sees in it only the prophecy of the English Bible), O'Casey has shown great foresight and done a singular service to Communism. In India and in many Asian countries the Christians are the first to turn Communists, in spite of being denounced at each step by their pastors. What if the message of the play reaches them and they realise that in being Communists they are only being good Christians? But the message will not reach them: the characters who speak it are dramatically dead. And there is too much death in the play.

If *Red Roses for Me* (1943) proves anything it is that

The Star Turns Red failed not because of the faith it
propagated but because it was poor drama. The background of the play, though not specifically stated, is the
Irish Transport Workers' strike of 1913; the hero is a
doomed idealist called Ayamonn Breydon, a Protestant,
in love with a Catholic girl, Sheila Moorneen. Ayamonn
lives with his mother in a dilapidated house in a working-
class locality in Dublin. Reading, painting, music,
theatre, all interest Ayamonn, but what most absorbs
him is the welfare of his brethren. A strike is organised
by the workers for a shilling-a-week increase in wages,
and Sheila begs him to take no part in it. But Ayamonn
turns a deaf ear to her entreaties, and in a clash with
the police is shot dead. Dying, he sends words to his
friend, the Parish Rector, the Rev. E. Clinton: ". . . this
day's but a day's work done, an' it'll be begun again
tomorrow."[12] To this thin plot are knit a number of
scenes and incidents which do not further the main
action but which add greatly to the overall beauty of
the play. The most charming of these is the tale of the
miserly but good-hearted landlord, Brennan, stealing
the soiled statue of Our Lady of Eblana and giving it a
new coat of paint, an event which is hailed as a miracle
by his simple and superstitious Catholic tenants.

In *Red Roses for Me*, O'Casey does not merely return
to Dublin for his *milieu* but uses a setting and characters
with which he is familiar. Like *The Shadow of a Gunman*,
the play is highly autobiographical. The first two acts
take place in the Breydon home, which is more or less
a picture of O'Casey's home in north Dublin. The third
act is set on the bridge spanning the river Liffey, and in
the fourth act the Church of St Burnupus is really the
Church of St Barnabas, very near to where O'Casey
lived while his mother was alive. Ayamonn is most
certainly the young Sean O'Casey as the old Sean
O'Casey recalled him; Mrs Breydon in her warmth,
charity, fellow-feeling, and courage resembles O'Casey's

mother; Sheila Moorneen is based on the Catholic girl Maura about whom O'Casey has written in *Inishfallen Fare Thee Well* in the chapter "The Girl He Left Behind Him"; the Rector embodies the qualities of the two priests for whom O'Casey had great respect, the Reverend Harry Fletcher and the Reverend E. M. Griffin, and about whom he writes in his autobiographies. The minor characters too are drawn from people O'Casey knew in his youth, and we find that certain dialogues are taken verbatim from *Pictures in the Hallway*, which appeared only a year before this play.

One can also trace in *Red Roses for Me* a number of features to be found in the Dublin trilogy. Slum life is depicted with all its accompanying poverty and hunger; there is the same lack of privacy as we saw in *The Shadow of a Gunman*; and any attempt on the part of the women to dress and live well is criticised by their neighbours. Apart from some difference in the external situation, the play has much in common with *The Plough and the Stars*. Sheila, like Nora, does all she can to keep Ayamonn away from the fight. Her entreaties, like Nora's, are brushed aside. Jack, however, fights to feed his vanity and personal ambition; Ayamonn, for the good of the workers. Both the heroes die. Nora is a finer character than Sheila for she is protecting her home against the folly of her husband, while the latter is trying to hold back her sweetheart from a fight for the general good. There are quarrels between Protestants and Catholics, between rationalists and believers. The third act, on the Liffey, like the second act of *The Plough and the Stars*, is a vignette: the former of Dublin as it then was, the latter of Dublin as it one day could be. However, the similarities end here. In *Red Roses for Me* O'Casey drives headlong towards the red horizon, and if for the best part of the evening we lose sight of the Party line it is because the dramatist in O'Casey has got the better of the propagandist.

Red Roses for Me censures the capitalists far more severely than *The Star Turns Red*, and it does so far more effectively. O'Casey changes his method of attack completely: instead of showing the wicked capitalists on the stage he shows the effect of their system on the masses. There are no Fascists with pistols in their holsters and no Jacks and Red Jims waving red flags and swearing at their opponents. There are only hungry people on the stage: "their faces are stiff and mask-like, holding tight an expression of dumb resignation; and are traversed with seams of poverty and a hard life."[13] All that they want is bread; all that the workers are fighting for is a shilling's increase in their weekly wages. They have been offered threepence instead! ". . . th' lowsers!" is how the 2nd Railwayman describes the employers to Ayamonn, and then turning to the Rector who is present, adds: " 'Scuse me, sir."[14] How far removed this is from the filthy invectives strewn over several pages of *The Star Turns Red* and Red Jim's immoderate demand:

LADY MAYORESS: What, in the name of God, do you want?
RED JIM: The World![15]

Of course, the shilling for which Ayamonn and the workers are fighting is symbolic, and it is not modesty that prevents them from asking for more. When the Inspector, the only representative of the capitalistic class and one who has a lot of good in him, advises Ayamonn not to risk his life for a shilling (for what can a shilling buy?), Ayamonn replies:

A shilling's little to you, and less to many; to us it is our Shechinah, showing us God's light is near; showing us the way in which our feet must go; a sun-ray on our face; the first step taken in the march of a thousand miles.[16]

In the end when Ayamonn is shot dead, the Inspector

tells Sheila that he did his best to save Ayamonn's life,
even tried to force his horse between the police and him.
In making his capitalists human O'Casey is not condoning
their inhumanity, but emphasising that the battle of
Communism is not against individuals but against a
system.

The same sense of balance and understanding of human
feelings brings the play to a soul-stirring conclusion.
Instead of letting the workers claim Ayamonn's body
and thunder formal praises over it, O'Casey has the bier
taken to the church where Mrs Breydon awaits it. The
mother and the priest speak softly:

RECTOR [*arranging a shawl round Mrs Breydon's shoul-
ders*]: There; that's better! My wife insists you stay the
night with us, so there's no getting out of it.

MRS BREYDON: She's kind. [*She pauses to look at the
rowan tree.*] There's th' three he loved, bare, or
dhrenched with blossom. Like himself, for fine things
grew thick in his nature: an' lather come the berries,
th' red berries, like the blood that flowed today out of
his white body. [*Suddenly—turning to face the church.*] Is
it puttin' out th' lights he is?

RECTOR: Yes, before he goes home for the night.

MRS. BREYDON: Isn't it a sad thing for him to be lyin'
lonesome in th' cheerless darkness of th' livelong
night!

RECTOR [*going to the porch and calling out*]: Sam, leave
the lights on tonight.

[*The church, which had dimmed, lights up again.*][17]

The most moving thing in the play is the expressionistic third act. The dull and dismal quays of Dublin,
crowded with listless men and women in drab-coloured
clothes, suddenly light up in the setting sun into mauve
and bronze as Ayamonn unfolds to them his dream of
the city's hidden splendour. A joyous melody played on
a flute is wafted abroad as Ayamonn dances out to meet

the girl Finnoola. The two dance opposite each other while the people clap their hands to the tap of the dancers' feet. The sun sets, the music ceases, the drabness reappears. Only the vision remains. The curtain coming down on the sound of marching feet and the revolutionary song—

> We swear to release thee from hunger and hardship,
> From things that are ugly and common and mean;
> Thy people together shall build a great city,
> The finest and fairest that ever was seen.—[18]

holds out hope that this dream may one day become a permanent reality.

Robert Hogan in his analysis of this act makes two objections: "The first is that nothing dramatic happens; the main action is derailed for the lyrical interlude. The second is that the scene, if it succeeds, succeeds by stage magic. The magic is not the magic of the dramatist, but that of the choreographer, the electrician, and the set designer."[19] To the first objection I would say that dramatically a lot happens: the people get their first dream-view of an Ireland they are fighting for, and it is for this Ireland that they lay down their lives. As for the second objection, certainly the scene succeeds because of stage magic. But it is O'Casey who writes the magic, and the choreographer and the electrician merely interpret it, very much as the actors interpret his glowing words. Also, if the act is totally in the hands of the stage technicians, then mere reading and visualising of it should convey nothing. I, for one, have not seen the play performed, but I have found it stimulating reading.

Red Roses for Me had its first London performance at the Embassy Theatre in February 1946, and its Broadway, New York, performance at the Booth Theatre in December 1955 (this was O'Casey's first full-length play to reach New York since *Within the Gates* twenty years earlier). The reception was on the whole mixed. Most critics praised the play for the splendour of its language, but regretted that the characterisation was not up to O'Casey's best and that structurally the play was weak. To take the question of language first, one cannot but admire the snatches of glorious poetry the like of which we have not had on the stage since Shakespeare. But like Shakespeare O'Casey is careless in distributing his words among the characters. One can understand the Shakespeare-drunk Ayamonn surrendering to high-flown rhetoric, and may even forgive him for such contrived utterances as "Time's a perjured jade, an' ever he moans a man must die," but it is a little too much to endure the police Inspector's eloquence. Here he is comforting Sheila after Ayamonn's death:

You'll see it clearer, dear, when busy Time in space has set another scene of summer's glory, and new-born spring's loud voice of hope hushes to silence th' intolerant dead.[20]

Hogan in his book has pointed out the play's structural faults. Almost half the drama is exposition and there are incidents that have little pertinence to the major plot. The quarrel between Ayamonn and Sheila in Act 1 is not resolved and reappears in Act 2, only to end as inconclusively. The main action in Act 4 is held up by the introduction of new characters, and the lowering of the curtains to signalise the passing of time between Ayamonn's death and his body being brought to the church is amateurish. O'Casey takes a long time to build up the climax and then it is an off-stage affair. There is too much religion and politics in the play, so that we get no more than a peep at the lovers. There is no conflict in Ayamonn's mind and his fervour for the good life makes him as insipid a character as the Dreamer in *Within the Gates* and Jack in *The Star Turns Red*. He stands, as Hogan says, "for what is noblest in O'Casey the man and dullest in O'Casey the dramatist."[21] In spite of these flaws the play still ranks very high in our present-day theatre.

Oak Leaves and Lavender (1946) has little or no plot. The time is the Battle of Britain, and all the three acts are set in a large room of Dame Hatherleigh's old manor house. War-time activity is suggested by the presence of black-out curtains, air-raid sirens, the sound of marching feet, and by the introduction of Home Guards, policemen, land girls, farmers, a coward, and a conscientious objector. All these characters tell on the nerves of Feelim O'Morrigun, Dame Hatherleigh's butler, who is in charge of the war preparations at the home front. Feelim's son, Drishogue, and Dame Hatherleigh's son, Edgar, have just got their wings and are having a riotous time with their girls Monica and Jennie respectively. The two boys are shot down; Jennie dies in an attempt to save Edgar from his burning plane (the most improbable of deaths in any of O'Casey's plays) while Monica finds comfort in carrying Drishogue's child in her womb. Dame Hatherleigh expresses the familiar O'Casey optimism: "We must all go soon. Our end makes but a beginning for others."[22]

This thin plot, filled out with many tiresome and irrelevant incidents, is neatly framed within a Prelude and an Epilogue. At the start and finish we see the ghosts of the manor's previous inhabitants dance stiffly to a minuet played on a piano. They lament the passing of England's old glory and express a fear of power being in the hands of the masses. The evil that is to befall the house is further presaged by the smell of lavender which becomes more insistent as the danger increases (O'Casey uses an old Cornish legend that the smell of lavender and the rustle of ghostly dancers are experienced in old houses when death approaches). However, the success of this scene lies solely in the stage directions that O'Casey gives and not in the words spoken by the ghostly dancers, most of which are in fact pretentious. When one of the Gentlemen Dancers asks another what had brought this sense of danger, he replies: "It comes from those who came from us, for England is at war."[23] Still, the Prelude and the Epilogue are well conceived, for they give the play a sort of unity; they also hint that England's heritage is worth defending and fighting for. O'Casey has a lot of praise for those who withstood the ordeal of the Battle of Britain, and patriotic Englishmen may think better of the play than I do.

Apart from the fine characterisation of Feelim, and a certain amount of skill in weaving dance, music, song, and humour into the structure of the play (which was done much better in *Red Roses for Me*), there is nothing to interest us even moderately. Drishogue, the spiritual descendant of the Dreamer, Jack, and Ayamonn, is as flat a character as one could conceive. He is a Communist, and we don't blame him for that; he has no love for England, and we are not bothered about that; he is fighting Nazi Fascism, and we applaud him for that; but he is a conceited and opinionated bore, and this we cannot forgive. Whenever he is on the stage, O'Casey so directs the flow of conversation that Drishogue may have the last say. Incidents and characters that have no relevance to the theme are dragged in so that the hero may air his views. A notable example is Mrs Deeda Tutting, who is brought in so that Drishogue may speak of the might of the Soviet Union. And this is what he tells her fiercely and loudly: "Woe unto any nation making war on the Soviet Union! She will slash open the snout, and tear out the guts of any power crossing her borders!"[24] Mrs Deeda Tutting, however, remains unimpressed and Drishogue gives up the argument, saying: "You waste God's time and mine, woman."[25] I shall take a hint from Drishogue and not waste my readers' time with this play.

Of the three Communistic plays, only *Red Roses for Me*

is successful drama. It is not that art dries up under Communism, we have Brecht to prove the contrary; the truth is that O'Casey allows his faith to get the better of the dramatist in him. With his firm belief in the rightness and nobility of his Communist heroes, he is unable to see their weaknesses and follies. O'Casey's political awakening has detracted something from the dramatist in him, and this can be seen not by comparing his Communistic plays with his Dublin plays but by observing that the best scenes in his Communistic plays are those where he momentarily forgets or sidetracks the political issue. Replying to Mr Kenneth Tynan's review of *Purple Dust*, O'Casey said: ". . . so when he's writing a play, the dramatist is neither Tory nor Communist, but only a playwright, setting down his characters as he knew them, giving, if he can, an added depth, height, and lilt to the words he makes them speak."[26] How one wishes O'Casey had followed his own precepts!

REFERENCES

1. *F.G.C.*, p. 95. A good study of O'Casey's early politics by Mr R. Ayling is included in *The Dubliner*, Spring 1964, pp. 54-67.
2. *F.G.C.*, p. 17.
3. *Creative Society*, 1935, p. 143.
4. *The Star Turns Red*, p. 353.
5. Krause, pp. 159-60.
6. Hogan, pp. 84-5.
7. *G.C.*, p. 66.
8. *How Not to Write a Play*, 1955, p. 67.
9. *The Star Turns Red*, p. 249.
10. *Op. cit.*, p. 296.
11. *Op. cit.*, pp. 324-5.
12. *Red Roses for Me*, p. 221.
13. *Op. cit.*, p. 136.
14. *Op. cit.*, p. 181.
15. *The Star Turns Red*, p. 348.
16. *Red Roses for Me*, p. 211.
17. *Op. cit.*, p. 227.
18. *Op. cit.*, p. 204.
19. Hogan, p. 94.
20. *Red Roses for Me*, p. 226.
21. Hogan, p. 91.
22. *Oak Leaves and Lavender*, p. 110.
23. *Op. cit.*, p. 9.
24. *Op. cit.*, p. 51.
25. *Op. cit.*, p. 52.
26. *Under a Colored Cap*, p. 263.

CHAPTER V

O'CASEY AND IRELAND

The group of plays we have just examined were moralities which were meant to be entertainments, and except for *Red Roses for Me* they failed as entertainment. The next group, comprising *Purple Dust*, *Cock-a-doodle Dandy*, *The Bishop's Bonfire*, *The Drums of Father Ned*, and *Behind the Green Curtain* (the title-play in a volume including two other short plays), are entertainments propounding a moral view. They are all set in "imaginary" Irish villages, and, among the other things they have in common, what stands out prominently is O'Casey's attack on the Irish clergy and Catholicism, and the state to which Ireland has been reduced. The Irish, especially the clergy, have protested vehemently against O'Casey's "villifying" Ireland and have argued that he was quite out of touch with the country as it is to-day. O'Casey, who left Dublin in 1926 and did not go back except for two brief visits, insisted that his portrayal was factual and that he had kept himself fully informed of life and events in Ireland through Irish newspapers[1] and through visitors from across the Irish Sea. Barring for the moment the question of who is right and who is wrong, at least two things are obvious: first, that these plays, in spite of the occasional rancour and bitterness that runs through them, are the work of a man profoundly in love with Ireland; second, that the Irish clergy have successfully kept most of the later O'Casey plays from reaching the Dublin stage.

A few fallacies should be removed. Much has been made of O'Casey's having been brought up as a Protestant in a predominantly Catholic country. This has often been used to show that O'Casey does not understand the Catholic religion and its practices, that he is unduly hard on people belonging to a different faith. This is not so: in the religious discussions in his plays between Protestants and Catholics, O'Casey takes no side, but condemns bigotry, superstition, intolerance, etc., wherever he meets them. If the Catholic clergy get a large measure of his wrath it is because O'Casey is writing of modern Ireland, and without the Catholic priest, to use a phrase of Sean O'Faolain, "any picture of modern Ireland is unthinkable."[2] Also, the Catholic clergy in Ireland owe much of their social prominence to political influence, and this influence has not always been used for the good of the people or for Irish freedom. Many of them opposed Nationalism, the teaching of Irish in the schools, and the Labour Movement: all at one time very dear to O'Casey. As O'Casey sees it, the priests are responsible for the poverty of the people, the lack of joy, late marriages, the censorship of books and films, and the large number of Irish emigrants. Above all they are against Communism: a reason good enough for O'Casey to come down upon them with full fury.

Vivian Mercier in *The Irish Comic Tradition* says that "The broad category of religious satire includes the most diverse treatments of a variety of themes: denunciations of apostasy, theological dissections of heresy, outcries against clerical materialism, and humorously Voltairian criticism of clerical celibacy and other even more fundamental tenets of Roman Catholicism."[3] One early anti-clerical work is Edward M'Nulty's *Mister O'Ryan* (1894), where the priest is shown as a vulgar, whiskey-loving, political intriguer. Thus O'Casey is not the first to satirise the priest or to question some Roman Catholic practices. His work is in the main stream of Irish literature, written both in Gaelic and English, of which the most striking single fact is the harsh vein of ridicule running through it. What is wrong with O'Casey's portrayal is that he has concentrated only on a small section of the clergy battening on the superstitions of an ignorant laity; in spite of the contrast he makes between good and bad priests, he has failed to convey that the majority of the priests are kind, good humoured, dedicated to their work, and loved and obeyed by the educated and the uneducated alike.

Purple Dust (1940) was published a few months after *The Star Turns Red*, but all that it has in common with the latter play are references to the Spanish Civil War and the one-dimensional characterisation. Basil Stoke and Cyril Poges, two rich English businessmen, acquire a tottering Tudor mansion in a village in the west of Ireland and prepare to settle down to the pleasures of country life with their mistresses Avril and Souhaun. They hire Irish workmen to redecorate the falling mansion, but it is not long before they discover the difficulty of transplanting themselves from the comforts of London to the primitiveness of the Irish countryside. Their manners, temperament, outlook, clash with those of the Irish, till the whole house becomes a bedlam. The two Irish girls get tired of their dull-witted, fussy Englishmen and are lured away by the romanticism and virility of the foreman, O'Killigain, and the Second Workman, O'Dempsey. The play ends with the river rising and flooding the house (the river is the river of Time sweeping away the remnants of a bygone age), and Poges wishing that he were back in England.

The play has its origin in two different sources: the plot is obviously derived from O'Casey's reading of Shaw's *John Bull's Other Ireland*; the best part of its poetry carries more than an echo of Synge's masterpiece, *The Playboy of the Western World*. Where language is concerned, however, O'Casey is as much a master as Synge and there are many passages which bear the O'Casey stamp.

Here I am particularly thinking of the scene where the workmen induce Poges to buy their hens:

1st WORKMAN [*persuasively—towards Poges' paper*]: Listen, here, sir: if it's genuine poulthry you want, that lay with pride an' animation, an' not poor, insignificant fowls that set about th' business o' layin' like a member o' Dolye Eireann makin' his maiden speech, I have a sthrain o' pullets that'll give you eggs as if you were gettin' them be steam!

POGES [*angrily—glancing over the top of his paper*]: Go away, go away, man, and don't be driving me mad!

3RD WORKMAN [*towards Poges' paper*]: Oh, the lies that some can tell to gain their own ends! Sure, sir, everyone knows that his poor hins are harmless; only venturin' to lay when heavy thunder frightens them into a hasty sign o' life! But it's meself can give you what you want, with a few lively cocks thrown in, to help them on with the work of furnishing nourishment to the whole world.[4]

In plot and characterisation, *Purple Dust* falls far short of *John Bull's Other Ireland*. Shaw's Englishmen are robust, lively, and full-blooded characters who, though at times absurd, are a match for their Irish counterparts. O'Casey's Englishmen are merely fools whose plight gets worse with every passing event, and who eventually lose their women and their home. Shaw's Broadbent can face up to the Irish and, in spite of all his comicality, score a point against them; O'Casey's Poges and Stoke are puppets who are bullied, cheated, and harassed and can do little but curse and moan. With the Irish characters, both O'Casey and Shaw are at home and easily depict their salient characteristics. O'Casey's success with his Irish characters, however, serves to heighten the inequality of the contest; in fact, there is little contest, for his Englishmen are no match for his Irish. The result is that O'Casey has to resort to theatrical tricks and knock-about farce to keep the play moving. Shaw's play has only one knock-about scene: the pig jumping into Broadbent's lap while he is driving his car. And this scene is brought in to make a very accurate observation. When Cornelius remarks that because of the incident Broadbent will lose his candidature for the parliamentary seat, Larry Doyle unerringly replies:

> Oh no he won't: hes not an Irishman. He'll never know theyre laughing at him; and while theyre laughing he'll win the seat.[5]

What observation has O'Casey to make in the numerous knock-about scenes he has introduced? None. Still, some of the scenes O'Casey has created are extremely amusing, specially those concerning the Yellow-Bearded Man breaking holes in the ceiling in the wrong places, and then comforting Poges: "Don't worry; just a little mistake in measurement, sir. Never fear, we'll hit th' right spot one o' these days!"[6] His reaction on hearing that Avril has ridden off on a horse stark naked is equally funny; so also is his indignation at Stoke's killing his innocent cow, thinking it to be a bull:

> Twenty-five pounds, an' not a penny less, he'll pay for it, or I'll have the heavy law on him. I'd ha' let you have her at first for the twenty, but in some compensation for th' agony of seein' the poor thing sink down into death, I'll have to get the other five, or I'll have the heavy law on him.[7]

Who but O'Casey could conceive such scenes? Who but O'Casey could write so well?

Among the gayest of O'Casey's comedies, and perhaps the mildest in its attack on the clergy (the clergyman makes but one brief entrance in Act III; still, his materialism and Puritanism are manifest), this play surely ought to have been produced by the Abbey Theatre. But the depiction of two Irish girls prostituting themselves for money is too strong an indictment for the taste of "holy Ireland," and the play has been successfully kept off the Dublin stage. O'Casey pays no homage to mere chastity: in his opinion it is commendable in the two women to leave the men who are mentally and physically sick for those who are healthy in mind and body. However, the play has had two notable productions in England: the first in 1945 and the other in 1962. Both productions were to some extent marred by unsatisfactory presentation and inadequate acting. The most successful run the play had was in New York in 1956. It ran for fourteen months, the longest run for an O'Casey play in the United States.

Cock-a-doodle Dandy (1949) was O'Casey's favourite play, and one that most sharply defines his views on Ireland in particular and life in general. The three scenes are set in Michael Marthraun's front garden. He is a small farmer, who is haggling over the price demanded by Sailor Mahon, the owner of a fleet of lorries, for carrying his turf from the bog to the village. From Michael we learn that sinister forces are at work in their village of Nyadnanave since Loreleen, his daughter by his first wife, has returned from England. An indomitable cock invades Michael's house, pecks at his tail-hat, claws the holy pictures, tosses down the delftware, and scares the wits out of people. Cups and saucers fly out of the window, the whiskey changes colour, and the chairs on which the two men are sitting collapse. Father Domineer, the parish priest, is sent for, and he with the help of the Police Sergeant, Michael, and One-Eyed Larry fight a fantastic battle against the evil invader. In the beginning the Cock gets the better of its opponents: it thrashes the priest, raises a wind that whips off the pants of the local constable, shakes the house as if in an earthquake and blows down the Irish flag. But Father Domineer, who shares some of the Cock's indefatigable qualities, summons his battered crew for a final lunge at the bird. Just then Loreleen is dragged in before the priest: she has been found about to make love to Sailor Mahon. Father Domineer rebukes her savagely for leading a "decent" man into "a scarlet sin" and banishes her to England. Lorna, Michael's second wife, the maid Marion, and the Messenger, all exponents of youth and sexual freedom, follow Loreleen into exile.

O'Casey's purpose may best be explained by the dramatist's own comment on the play in *The New York Times*:

> The play is symbolic in more ways than one. The action manifests itself in Ireland, the mouths that speak are Irish mouths; but the spirit is to be found in action everywhere: the fight made by many to drive the joy of life from the hearts of men; the fight against this fight to vindicate the right of the joy of life to live courageously in the hearts of men.[8]

All this is very fine thought, but O'Casey does not take us beyond what he has reiterated in play after play since *Within the Gates*. A lot of miracles have occurred on the stage, but none in terms of the theatre.

The Cock is O'Casey's symbol of joy, courage, sexual ecstasy, and vibrant living. To the village philistines it is the very incarnation of the devil, but for Loreleen and the Messenger it holds no terrors. It comes closest to Loreleen, who in her way of living embodies all that the Cock stands for. In fact the two are indivisible: the one is the body, the other the spirit. And it is for this reason that the two are never shown on the stage at the same time. Father Domineer, who knows that "th' biggest fight th' holy saints ever had was with temptations from good-lookin' women,"[9] happily banishes Loreleen, and does not regret Lorna and Marion joining her. Lorna's and Marion's position is not clear in the beginning, for the two women waver between the pietistic teachings of their priest and their own inner urge for a fuller life.

But it is not long before they start living according to the dictates of their consciences, thereby siding with the Cock. It is the priest and his Puritanical crew who wage an all-out battle with the Cock, and this battle is the comic highlight of the play.

There are a couple of incidents without which the play would have been the better. The first concerns the priest accidentally smiting a man dead. There was such a case in Ireland, but O'Casey completely fails to integrate it into the play. Moreover, the tragic development deprives the play of its comedy and makes it unnecessarily brutal. To an intelligent audience it is not a priest killing a man but O'Casey killing the play. The second incident is dramatically no less a failure than the first. Julia, Michael's sister-in-law, leaves for Lourdes for a cure at the end of Scene I and returns unhealed at the end of Scene III, to renounce her faith in miracles. O'Casey makes pathetic attempts to fuse the incident into the main body of the play, but in vain. What is even more irritating is the question: how could a woman leave a remote Irish village for Lourdes in the morning and return home the same evening? Though the stage directions do not say that the play is set in a single day, everything else indicates that this is so. One might argue that in a fantasy a critic ought not to consult the railway time-table but the scene is realistic and realistically treated. In both incidents, O'Casey has clearly gone out of his way to have a thrust at the clergy and to ridicule Catholic faith in Saints and miracles. And he has emerged the poorer for it. Dublin will have nothing to do with this play; and the few performances it has had elsewhere, including the one at the Edinburgh International Festival in 1959, more than hint that the very best of an Irish cast is required to do justice to the characterisation, the fine snatches of dialogue, and much racy fooling that O'Casey has provided. But where except in Dublin could we expect to find the right cast?

The over-all picture of life in Ireland that O'Casey gave in *Cock-a-doodle Dandy* was a grim one, and the same grim view underlies his next play *The Bishop's Bonfire* (1955). Hectic preparations are being made to receive Bishop Bill Mullarkey in his home town of Ballyoonagh. Count Reiligan, who is also a Councillor and the richest man in the district, and Canon Burren, the parish priest, are anxious to make the Bishop's visit a memorable one, and, among other plans to celebrate the occasion, have decided on a bonfire in which bad books and evil pictures shall be burned. The play opens with the workmen redecorating Reiligan's house (where the Bishop is to stay), and creating confusion and chaos somewhat similar to that in *Purple Dust* and in the last act of *The Star Turns Red*. The preparation for the visit is the main theme, and supplies all the comedy element in the play. To this theme are skilfully knit two tragic sub-plots: the love of Reiligan's workmen for their employer's daughters. Manus Moanroe's love for Foorawn is frustrated by the latter's vow of chastity, and Daniel Clooncoohy's love for Keelin is smothered by the Count and the Canon because of class distinctions. The play ends with Manus Moanroe shooting Foorawn, when she is about to call the police on discovering that he is decamping with a bundle of stolen currency notes. Robert Hogan has described this scene as "one of the best that O'Casey has written since the death of Bessie Burgess."[10] However, the majority of critics have strongly disapproved of it on the grounds that it is melodramatic, unnecessarily brutal, and unconvincing.

A lesser work than *Cock-a-doodle Dandy*, *The Bishop's Bonfire* touches on most of the problems raised in the earlier play. There is the question of exile: Manus, a lapsed priest who has served in the R.A.F., must, like Loreleen, return to England, for life in Ireland is unbearable. In the exile of his characters one can see the story of O'Casey's own exile: he too had to leave a land

where joy, love, and life were not his birthright. In both
plays we see the Church and the State leagued together
to fill the mind of man with a superstitious fear of life
and a distrust of happiness. O'Casey is fair in not putting
the blame on the Church alone, but insisting that
the individual is in the wrong for tolerating and even
siding with institutions that are responsible for his
misery. There is the vigorous attack on beliefs in Saints
and miracles: everything in Irish life is on the decrease
except the number of holy images. However, this attack
is dramatically feasible: it springs from the plot and is
not grafted on it like the Julia-Lourdes episode in
Cock-a-doodle Dandy.

One question that arises is whether life in present-day
Ireland is as bad as O'Casey depicts it in his plays. A
few Irish Catholic critics have argued that the dramatist
is behind the times, that the Ireland shown in the plays
is long since dead, and that the priests are no longer a
power in the land. O'Casey in his article "Bonfire Under
a Black Sun"[11] denies these charges and maintains that
his is a faithful portrayal of what is currently happening
in Ireland. The truth, however, lies somewhere between
the two extremes. Life in Ireland has improved con-
siderably in recent years: there has been a proliferation
of dance halls; the average age of marriage for men and
women, though still the highest in Europe, has dropped
a little; emigration has steadily decreased from an
average of 40,000 to 20,000 in 1963. The clergy remain
as powerful as O'Casey shows them, and nothing short
of this could have prevented his plays from reaching
Dublin. They have imposed a rigorous censorship
on books and films that raise awkward questions, and
there is not an Irish writer of repute one or more of
whose works have not been banned in Ireland. Still, the
majority of the priests are humane and not as they are
presented in the plays. This does not mean that there
are no priests in Ireland like Canon Burren; there are,

>ut they are few. The best summary of the play from
:he priests' viewpoint was made by a Catholic prelate
:o whom Cyril Cusack sent *The Bishop's Bonfire* before
)roducing it in Dublin. The prelate wrote:

My immediate reaction is one of regret that you have
decided to put it on. Of course it is good theatre;
anything of Sean O'Casey would be that. But the
bitterness that runs through all his plays and his scorn
of the Church and of religious practice vitiate his
art. . . . I know there are ecclesiastics rather like the
Canon, and prominent Catholics like the Count;
there may even be priests like the curate; and all of
them are distasteful and deserved to be pilloried. But
are all Parish Priests as blind as the Canon (to put it
no worse) or as ignorant as the curate? Are all "good"
laymen as unChristian as the Count, all "good"
women as hypocritical as Foorawn? Is it only drunkards
and ne'er-do-wells that have the vision of the truth?
Is all prayer to be sneered at and the intercession of
the Saints a thing for mockery?[12]

This is, I must reiterate, a priest's point of view and far
removed from O'Casey's own vision of good and bad.
The curate, for instance, is the dramatist's ideal of a
priest, but to the prelate he is as obnoxious as the Canon
and the Count. This seems to leave no common ground
where O'Casey and the Irish clergy could meet. As a
consequence one of the greatest dramatists in the
English language has been shunned in his own country.
Could there have been a greater tragedy for this master
of comedy?

The rejection of *The Drums of Father Ned* (published
1960) after it had been accepted for production at the
Dublin International Theatre Festival in 1958 (the
Festival was to be a part of the An Tostal, or Spring
Celebration) was the shabbiest treatment O'Casey
received from his native city. The Tostal Council had

selected the O'Casey play, along with Joyce's *Ulysses* (dramatised by Alan McClelland and called *Bloomsday*) and three mime plays of Samuel Beckett. The Archbishop of Dublin indicated his disapproval of the choice of plays by refusing to open the Tostal with the celebration of an official Mass. The Tostal Council, frightened by the Archbishop's stand and the pressure brought by the public, came out with the excuse that O'Casey's play would need some structural changes before it could be performed. O'Casey quickly sensed what the matter was and withdrew his play. All right-minded people the world over sympathised with O'Casey, regretted the step taken by the Archbishop, and condemned the Tostal Council for its lack of courage and integrity. O'Casey retaliated by withdrawing from the Abbey and the other theatres in Ireland the permission to produce his plays.[13]

The Drums of Father Ned is not a great play, but it is a successful summing up of O'Casey's technical achievements and convictions. With much skill he has woven into an intricate whole such diverse elements as fantasy, farce, melodrama, satire, symbolism, realism, dance, music, song, and colour. Angus's Bird has the colours of the various symbols handled in the earlier plays: black for the priesthood; red for Communism; green for Ireland; crimson and gold for life, but more too, since gold is O'Casey's favourite colour. The problems raised in his earlier plays are all there; there is not, however, the despair of *Cock-a-doodle Dandy* and *The Bishop's Bonfire*. The plot has a close resemblance to that of the latter play: there is the preparation, not for a bishop but for the Tostal Celebrations; the priest, in the title role, like Bishop Mullarkey, does not appear. There are the old kill-joys, aided and abetted by a restrictive priest, ranged against young people standing for love, sex, and freedom. But they do not succeed. Youth's victory is proclaimed through the lovers Nora and Michael standing for the Dail election, and the sound of Father Ned's drums.

There are also in the play references to Communism; arguments between Catholics and Protestants in favour of their respective religions; and youth, especially young women, giving affirmation to the dramatist's most cherished values.

What is new in the play is the "Prerumble": a flashback set in the Ireland of the 1920s. As the town burns, some Black and Tans amuse themselves by plaguing two Irishmen who hate each other more than they hate the British. This hatred saves their lives, for the two are let off in the hope that they "will do more harm to Ireland living than they'll ever do to Ireland dead."[14] Though I do not share Robert Hogan's enthusiasm for the play, I do agree with him that this scene is "one of the sparest, most telling and grimly grotesque single pieces that O'Casey has ever written."[15] It alone makes the play a worthwhile effort.

In *Behind the Green Curtains* (1961) O'Casey belabours the Irish intelligentsia for their ingrained cowardice and lack of convictions. A poet, an artist, an actor, a gossip-column writer, together with their patron Chatastray— an industrialist, speak up in private ("behind green curtains") for freedom and the rights of man, but tremble before the correspondent of *The Catholic Buzzer* and the orders of the Bishop. One result of their cowardice is that an innocent girl, Noneen, is accused of immorality, pilloried by the laymen who have the priest's approval, and has to flee with the atheist-Communist Beoman to England. (I wonder why O'Casey never banished his Communists to Russia!) The incident proves an eye-opener to Reena, a young Catholic nurse belonging to the Legion of Mary, who follows Beoman into exile, but not before she has tried and failed to make Chatastray shake off the man-made shackles that bind him. The love scene between Reena and Beoman with which the play ends is unnatural; also, the opening scene where two middle-aged women try to identify the bearded man in the picture, though amusing, contributes little to the main action of the play. In theme and characterisation the play bears some resemblance to P. V. Carroll's *The White Steed* (1938) which possibly influenced it.

For the first time since *Within the Gates* we see characters torn by mental conflict—and how much richer the play is for that. Reena fights and wins—all glory to her; Chatastray loses, for he has not the strength in him to defy those instructions that have moulded his life. O'Casey censures him, but with sympathy and understanding. When Reena tells Chatastray that the sash (symbolic here of bigotry and fear) is no longer their concern, Chatastray replies:

> Of course not; all th' same, Reena, I'm thirty-five years old, an' this sash is a symbol of all I believe an' all th' customs I'm used to throughout them years.[16]

The emotions aroused when Chatastray leaves Reena to join the anti-Communist procession are similar to those aroused in *The Plough and the Stars*, when Jack leaves Nora to march away with his comrades-in-arms. There is pity, grief, regret, but no hate. This absence of hate and bitterness greatly contributes to the play's success, and not O'Casey's loud cry for the good life.

The other two plays included in the volume are *Figuro in the Night* and *The Moon Shines on Kylenamoe*. In the former, written in two scenes and dedicated to "The Ferocious Chastity of Ireland," O'Casey fires off a fusillade at Irish Puritanism and sings of pagan freedom with a vengeance. The nude statue of a boy puts the Dubliners in a frenzy and provides the dramatist with an opportunity for some excellent quips:

> 2ND OLD MAN: There was the Legion of Mary wailing their prime right to let go to the front to form a poster-ring of protection to prevent anyone wearing a skirt from seeing what would demolish every idea

in every girlish heart to ever again carry a cross for Ireland.

YOUNG MAN: They should let the girls look at it long enough to tire of it, I say.

2ND OLD MAN: Jimmy, Jimmy, what if they never tired of it? What in God's name are you thinking of?[17]

It is a great pity that Alan Simpson, because of certain cuts demanded by the Lord Chamberlain, was unable to produce this play at the festival of Irish comedy in July 1963. If ever a play deserved performance, here is one.

Because of pressure on space I have not discussed O'Casey's one-act plays,[18] though at least two of them, *Hall of Healing* and *The Moon Shines on Kylenamoe*, are good enough to be included even in the most sophisticated anthology. The latter, which bears some resemblance to *Purple Dust*, is a farcical comedy set in a lonely Irish railway station at night. Lord Leslieson of the British Foreign Office alights from the train and wishes to be directed to the town of Kylenamoe. "What town?" ask the Signalman and the Guard. They know of none. Confusion mounts. The only conveyance available is a donkey creel-cart, and not even that to begin with. Says the proud owner of the donkey:

I'm not goin' to rouse little Jinnie out of her donkey-dhreams, no, not for any England's great Prime Ministhers, or for any sthruttin' High Official of England's Foreign Office! [*More vehemently*] I'm tellin' yous I wouldn't molest little Jinnie out of her present repose if it was th' Parish Priest of Kylenamoe aself that was askin' me to do it![19]

Gabriel Fallon tells us that "Railway working had a fascination for him [O'Casey] and he actually played with the idea of writing a play called *The Signal*."[20] The rich characterisation, vivid dialogue, detached portrayal, and the fairness with which he hands out repartee left and right belong to the great Dublin trilogy.

Re-reading all that I have written, I find I have been hard on O'Casey and have dismissed at least one of his plays as unworthy of serious consideration. My plea must be that I have been judging O'Casey by the highest norm, and this norm has been supplied by O'Casey himself in plays such as *The Plough and the Stars* and *Within the Gates*. O'Casey undoubtedly suffers when his lesser works are compared with the best he has written, although even his worst plays have in them moments of real dramatic interest. Nathan in his foreword to *Five Great Modern Irish Plays* asks:

> Where in the drama of living Irishmen is there greater and more genuine dramatic poetry than you will find in the mighty sweep of *The Plough and the Stars*, or in the boozy low measures of *Juno*, or in the riff-raff of *Within the Gates* and their periodic utterance, or in the speech of the workmen in *Purple Dust*, or even in passages of the otherwise largely dubious *The Star Turns Red*?[21]

The answer is: nowhere. There are plays in which O'Casey will bore you stiff, and just when you are about to give him up as hopeless he will strike a note or a sentiment which will require you to re-examine your opinion. Nothing is more irritating to a professional critic than this; nothing confuses him more than spasmodic brilliance that throws all his conclusions to the winds.

One more point: O'Casey has been blamed for losing some of his dramatic force after exiling himself. For me, it is true that he reached his meridian in *The Plough and the Stars*, but there is nothing to support the view that had he stayed on in Dublin he would have repeated his success. On the contrary there are reasons to believe that in the provincial Dublin atmosphere his genius might have been confined to portraying the tenement world in all its frustrations, and his reputation might have declined from uniformity and surfeit. Such plays as *Within the Gates* and *The Silver Tassie* would in all probability never have been written, and to-day we have a body of critics—abler and more competent than myself —who feel that these two plays and not *The Plough and the Stars* is his greatest achievement. Leaving to the reader to decide which is O'Casey's greatest play, I have just this to ask of those who feel that O'Casey lost some of his force after his exile: in what way is *The Moon Shines on Kylenamoe* (apart from the limitations common to most one-acters) inferior to any other play O'Casey has written in his long dramatic career?

REFERENCES

1. See "Bonfire Under a Black Sun" in *G.C.*
2. *The Irish* (Penguin), 1947, p. 107.
3. *The Irish Comic Tradition*, 1962, p. 129.
4. *Purple Dust*, p. 32-3.
5. *John Bull's Other Island and Major Barbara*, 1907, p. 86.
6. *Purple Dust*, p. 43.
7. *Op. cit.*, p. 82.
8. "O'Casey's Credo," *The New York Times*, 9 Nov. 1958, Reprinted in *Playwrights on Playwriting*, ed. Toby Cole, 1960.
9. *Cock-a-doodle Dandy*, p. 125.
10. Hogan, p. 128.
11. *G.C.*, pp. 122-45.
12. Quoted in Cowasjee, p. 226.
13. For a detail account see Hogan, pp. 129-35; Cowasjee, pp. 231-4; Krause, pp. 212-21.
14. *The Drums of Father Ned*, p. 10.
15. Hogan, p. 136.
16. *Behind the Green Curtains*, p. 78. For a brief but good study of O'Casey's last plays, see William A. Armstrong, "The Irish Point of View" in *Experimental Drama*, 1963.
17. *Figuro in the Night* in *Behind the Green Curtains*, p. 110.
18. I have discussed these in my previous book.
19. *The Moon Shines on Kylenamoe* in *Behind the Green Curtains*, p. 147.
20. "The House on the North Circular Road," *Modern Drama*, 4, Dec. 1961, p. 230. See also *Sean O'Casey: the Man I Knew*, 1965, pp. 44-5.
21. *Five Great Modern Irish Plays*, 1941, p. xii.

CHAPTER VI

AUTOBIOGRAPHIES

O'Casey's prose works bulk larger than his plays. Four short stories, his first prose writing after his exile, were published in *Windfalls* (1934), a volume which in addition to the stories contained poems and two one-act plays. In 1937 there came *The Flying Wasp*, which consists of a series of essays giving the author's opinions on the London theatre and its critics. At least two figures are singled out for vigorous attack: the fashionable playwright Noel Coward and the equally fashionable critic James Agate. Though O'Casey has some legitimate reasons to complain, he errs through excess of vituperation. He devotes three chapters to Coward, and though there is some fair criticism the piece would have been better omitted. He quotes copiously from the observations of the London critics, and with shrewd comments of his own makes them look pretty silly. This volume was followed by the dramatist's life story in six volumes, published between 1939 and 1954. In 1956 appeared *The Green Crow*, which, in addition to articles and stories published earlier, contained some fresh material. Reviewing the volume, Henry Popkin said:

The constant burden of these essays is that O'Casey is right, that he has always been right, that practically everyone else except Shakespeare and Shaw is wrong, that his plays are right, too; and if he had a dog, his dog would be right. His tone as an essayist is reminiscent of the pugnacious cries of indignation we hear from some of his more wrathful characters, but

O'Casey has a gift for sustained indignation that puts
Fluther Good and the Covey to shame. Sustaining a
high pitch of rage for several pages is only one of his
feats of endurance; sustaining it for several years is
another.[1]

O'Casey's last published work is *Under a Colored Cap*
(1963), which the author described as a volume of
"Articles Merry and Mournful with Comments and a
Song." Most of the articles are neither merry nor
mournful but strong, bitter denunciation of official
Christianity, of critics who have failed to see eye to eye
with him, of writers like Auden and Arnold Toynbee
and others for whom he has a particular distaste. The
best thing in the book and as good as anything O'Casey
has ever written in prose is the story of Waxy, the
paralysed "kidger," who was the Commanding Officer
of the Inisfalliners in which Johnny of the autobiographical volumes served when he himself was a kid.
Waxy, who had a gift for making coloured caps for his
troops, "banjaxed" their last campaign by dying a
couple of days before what would have been a certain
victory. He went to his grave without his general's hat.
Johnny and his friends wanted it to be buried with him,
but Waxy's mother gently nudged them towards the door,
forgave them because they were Protestants, and hoped
that when they grew up they would have more sense.

O'Casey's chronicle of his life and times in six volumes
is surely his grandest achievement in prose. It is, as one
reviewer put it, "one of the most astonishing and
appalling documents of poverty, failure, success, and then
the poverty and failure of success itself, written in the
last half century."[2] A few critics feel that O'Casey's
reputation may ultimately rest on the autobiographies
rather than on the plays. This may not happen, but it
still indicates what an amazing achievement the autobiographies are. The approximate periods covered by

the volumes are: *I Knock at the Door* (1939), 1880-1891;
Pictures in the Hallway (1942), 1892-1904; *Drums under the
Window* (1946), 1905-1916; *Inishfallen Fare Thee Well*
(1949), 1916-1926; *Rose and Crown* (1952), 1926-1934;
Sunset and Evening Star (1954), 1934-1952. The autobiographies were made available in two volumes under the
title *Mirrors in My House* in 1956. It was chiefly from the
sale of the autobiographies rather than of the plays that
O'Casey was able to make a modest living. His integrity
often came in the way of his prosperity, and in *The
Green Crow* he tells us how he refused an offer of well over
$50,000 for doing a screenplay of Thomas Wolfe's *Look
Homeward, Angel* because he did not approve of Holly-
wood methods.

O'Casey writes of himself in the third person, no doubt
following his instinct as a dramatist. Though this may
be rather an unusual method for an autobiography, it
has several advantages: it frees him from the ubiquitous
personal pronoun "I," gives the work the dimension and
scope of a novel, and allows him to express opinions
without sounding egoistic. The fiction form must have
appealed strongly to him and this explains his scorn
for dates. One looks in vain for the date of his mother's
death, those of his meetings with Lady Gregory, Yeats,
Shaw, and others. He writes at length and with great
force on the many political events with which Dublin was
seething before Independence, but gives little evidence
to help us to place the events in their proper sequence.

Because of the third-person narration and the lack of
dates, many readers come to the conclusion that these
books are in no sense factual histories. In fact, they are
as factual as most histories and autobiographies. David
H. Greene writes:

There is also a lack of dependence upon fact—
Matthew Arnold once noted the Celt's disposition in
this regard—which is not to say that O'Casey makes

free with the truth but that he breathes life—a more important ingredient than fact—into it. Where facts are literally vital, as in his account of his row with Yeats over the rejection of *The Silver Tassie* or the hilarious account of Shaw's standing security for him when he rented a house in Devonshire, he can be fulsome. But even here he is still more interested in the dramatic rather than the historical elements of his material.[3]

O'Casey is much too clever to stick to mere facts. Nor does he expect us to believe that everything happened exactly as narrated. Take, for example, the scene where Johnny, after being caned mercilessly and unjustly by the schoolmaster Slogan, is made to stand up on a chair:

> Rapping on his desk with a heavy, glossy ebony ruler, Slogan silenced the murmur of the school. He put down the ruler on the desk beside him, and bent his hoary oul' head, saying softly, Let us pray.
>
> There was a clatter of moving bodies as all got down on to their knees. Slogan knelt down too, resting his hoary oul' head on his arms that rested on the seat of the chair from which he had risen to pray. The ebony ruler lay motionless on the desk beside him. O Lord, open Thou our eyes that we may behold wonderful things out of Thy law. The ebony ruler lay quiet on the desk beside him. Our Father which art in heaven. Hallowed be Thy Name.[4]

Johnny saw the pink, bald head of Slogan bent in prayer. He got down from the chair, picked up the heavy ruler, and brought it down with all the hate in his heart on the head of the teacher, and fled.

This account is no mere wish-fulfilment—such an incident could easily have happened. What the dramatist has done is to breathe new life into it. The prayer is an ironic comment on all that Slogan stands for. "O Lord, open Thou our eyes that we may behold wonderful

H

things out of Thy law" is quickly answered, but not as Slogan would have wished it. With a dramatist's intuition of proper timing and a skilful use of repetition, he brings about the desired effect. "The ebony ruler lay motionless on the desk beside him." And a sentence later: "The ebony ruler lay quiet on the desk beside him." The ruler was quiet and motionless, as if it were possible for it to be anything else! But there is an ominous quality about it and our attention, as that of Johnny, is riveted to it. O'Casey is a master of prose and handles the language with an ease and vigour approached by few contemporaries. He uses a variety of styles: when roused he can be Biblical, Shakespearian, Joycian; he can be lyrical, sentimental, rhetorical, or argumentative, as the occasion demands. Above all he is, as Richard Findlater puts it, "a magnificent wordspinner." His autobiographies are full of glorious puns, malapropisms, comic invective, and needle-sharp observations. However, his writing is uneven and at times he is exasperatingly long-winded and pseudo-poetic; he will shout when he ought to speak softly, and is too frequently carried away by the sound and rhythm of his words. Yet the reader gladly puts up with all this, not only because the best has no parallel but also because the force of the man is evident through all his writing. His is a style which is intensely private and personal.

There are, no doubt, a few factual errors in the autobiographies. To point out one, the impression that he leaves in *Inishfallen Fare Thee Well* and *Rose and Crown* is that he never visited Ireland after he left for England in 1926. This is not so. O'Casey himself acknowledged in a letter to me dated 31 Mar. 1959:

This is also a mistake. Came back to get books and papers. Stayed the night in a hotel opposite station for boat-train, and left first thing in the morning.

In fact he was in Ireland twice again. But what is

significant is that O'Casey should use the word "mistake." Surely, if this is a work of fiction an omission of this nature cannot be called a mistake, but O'Casey's use of the word clearly indicates that he does not wish his autobiographies to be accepted as fiction. His belittling the insurrectionary leaders and literary figures whose policies, works, or attitudes he could not accept does not turn the work into fiction either. We are free to disagree with him; even to surmise, and in many cases rightly, that the immediate spleen of the man gets the better of his judgment. However, these books are not written to serve the purpose of history—of such we already have enough. Present wisdom is not O'Casey's purpose, but it is to re-create in exuberant prose the impressions people and events left on his sensitive mind.

Of the six books, the first four about the raw Dublin poverty are the best. It is not surprising that he had once thought of concluding his life story with *Inishfallen Fare Thee Well*,[5] for anything following the account of his struggle with abject poverty to his rise to fame with the success of *The Plough and the Stars* was sure to arrive as an anticlimax. *I Knock at the Door* takes us from O'Casey's birth to the age when he was eleven and had first kissed a girl. Every incident is dramatised: Johnny's predecessor dying in his mother's arms as she waits in vain for the doctor to arrive; his father's death and funeral; his sister Ella going off to wed her bugler Nicholas without a word from her mother; the torture Johnny suffers from the pain in his eyes and the primitive cure he is subjected to; the "Battle Royal" between the school's big bullies and Johnny's friend and champion, Middleton; and much else. There is the same superb mingling of the serious and the comic that is found in his Dublin plays. Here is a scene from the chapter "His Father's Funeral"— the hearse drivers are waiting for the coffin:

Johnny, standing by the heads of the hearse horses,

saw the boy Connor, who went to school with him, standing beside his mother, watching him, and leering whenever he caught Johnny's eye. Johnny moved nearer to him so that Connor could get a better view of him standing cockily near the hearse horses, impatiently scraping the road with their feet and shaking the black plumes whenever they tossed their heads. Connor moved till he was just beside Johnny, though, sly enough, he held on to his mother's skirt, which he had stretched out as far as it could go. Johnny felt his head beside his shoulder, and heard him whisper in his ear, Go an' put your hand on a horse if you're as brave as you're thryin' to look.

Johnny stiffened with pride and stroked the band of crisp crêpe on his arm as he saw kids in the crowd watching him and Connor. Stretching out a hand timorously, he stroked the haunch of the nearest horse. The animal gave a shuddering start, and kicked viciously, making the hearse shake and Johnny jumped away from him in fright.

—Gaaaa, you mischeevous little bastard, roared the driver wearing the yellow muffler, gaaaa, out o' that, an' leave th' animal alone, or I'll go over an' kick the little backside off you!

Johnny slunk away a little, and turned his back to Connor, so that his shamed and frightened face couldn't be seen.

—Fifteen pints between eight and eleven, said the driver wearing the bowler hat, I wouldn't ask anything better, even on the night of me first daughter's weddin'. We got home, he went on, we got home, but it took two hours to do it, where it should ha' taken only twenty minutes: two solid hours o' mighty sthrivin', but we done it in the end.

—They ought to have the old man warmly folded up be this, said the man wearing the yellow muffler, didderay didderee didderum. [6]

The same ribaldry of Dublin's spoken prose runs through the next two volumes, and there is an even more daring mixture of styles and moods.

Pictures in the Hallway opens with Parnell's coffin arriving in Dublin and ends with Johnny throwing up his third job. Some seven chapters are devoted to his first job, which he got at the age of fourteen. The starting salary was three shillings and sixpence a week and the hours of work were from eight in the morning till six in the evening. Johnny now and again managed to steal a few minutes from his work—this ranged from running errands to sweeping the floors—to educate himself; with equal success he managed to pilfer small household articles for himself and his vanman. It was not long before he was out of a job for protesting strongly against a fine of two shillings imposed on him for impertinence and disobedience. His next job in the large firm of Jason and Son [Eason and Son], wholesale newspaper, stationery, and book dealers came to an equally abrupt end when he refused to take off his cap while receiving his wages. The third job, a temporary one, for "five hours' work on five days of the week for five shillings a week," did not prove much of a success either and he left it to work with pick and shovel at a railway siding.

With O'Casey, the ugly in deeds are invariably ugly in looks. He sketches those he dislikes with severity; the keen eye of the dramatist is always there, and the comedy is never lost sight of. He describes his second employers, father and son, thus:

The smaller figure of his son showed himself a thinner copy of the fat father, the big head, the smoky glitter of the eyes, the bitter brows, the splendidly circular legs, covered in knickerbockers and thin black cotton stockings. Both of them perpetually wore conceited grins, ever putting a jaunty air into their waddling, evidently finding a lot wrong with the straighter legs, normal heads, and natural necks of most other poor men.[7]

Equally sharp is his description of the ganger, Christy Mahon, whom Johnny disliked:

Mahon was another big and powerful man of fifty or so, wide-shouldered and deep-chested; lazy as sin, and as ignorant as a kish of brogues. . . . There was one remarkable thing about him—he had a very small arse for such a big man, and the part of his trousers there looked like the drooping mainsail of a ship in a fitful wind when he walked.[8]

There is the rich dialogue, comparable with the best to be found in his plays. Here is one of his employers selling his goods to old Biddy, who deals in cracked china:

—Now, now, Biddy, be fair; be just. Have another look at it, said the figure, gently rocking on its toes. There's a fine heap of fair goods there, really. And you can have it all for twelve and six—not a farthing less.

—Arra, Mr. Anthony, your poor eyes must be seein' double this evenin', the hot sun havin' affected them, or somethin'. Twelve an' six, is it, you said? Is it a silver mine you think I have undher the stable where I keep th' animal? Fine heap d'ye call it? An' next to nothin' in it that's more than ready to fall asundher, if you blew a cold breath on them. . . . Looka th' pots—you'll have to hold your hands undher them the whole time th' thing's cookin'.

—Now, Biddy, Biddy, don't exaggerate. The cracks go barely half-way down the saucepans. With a little care in handling, they'll serve the poor people excellently, excellently. It looks the best, it is the best lot yet you've had before you. Come, now, be reasonable: say ten shillings, then?[9]

This, as well as much else in the earlier volumes, could be effectively staged. In fact the first two volumes have had some successful stage readings.

Pictures in the Hallway is also important for the light it throws on O'Casey's interest in the theatre since his very boyhood. Even before he could read or understand Shakespeare, he was spouting lines from *Henry VI* for a charity concert. Later, when his brother Archie and a friend formed the Townshend Dramatic Society, he acted in the plays of Shakespeare and Boucicault, and other dramatists included in Dick's *Standard Plays*. "Boucicault was the boyo to choose," thought young Johnny then, and the old Johnny did not change his opinion as is evident from the melodrama in his own plays. Another thing noticeable in the book is that his Da's and Ma's opinions, which were prominent in *I Knock at the Door*, are gradually making way for his own. Though Johnny is still modest, we can see that he is on the road where no one's opinions but his own will matter.

In *Drums Under the Window* we see a turbulent Dublin —prior to and during the years which bore bitter issue in the Easter Rebellion of 1916—through the eyes of Johnny, who has changed his name to Sean:

Themes are opposed: the penury and squalor of the Dublin poor is set against the dream of a resurgent Ireland; Sean labors with pick and shovel to keep a family in dry bread and tea and attends the classes of the Gaelic League, where the Ireland of the heroes and poets is made known to him; the lonely death of his brother, his sister's husband's madness and death, her eviction with her children and their settlement in his poverty-stricken domicile are set against the pageant of resurgent Gaeldom; his own threatened paralysis against the founding of the Citizen Army and the National Volunteers.[10]

The book has been criticised for its attack on religion,

its historical bias, and its disparagement of certain
political leaders. No doubt it contains a trenchant
criticism of both Catholic and Protestant clergy for their
disregard of the needs of the poor; the Catholic clergy
in addition are denounced for their political manoeuvring,
as in the issue of the compulsory teaching of Irish in the
universities. The book is not the final judgment of a
mature man on religion, but it is what Sean thought of
God and Man at a time of personal and national tragedy.
As for the historical bias and disparaging statements,
they are there for all those who see men and events in
a different light from O'Casey himself. I believe he does
injustice to Captain J. R. White, Arthur Griffith,
Douglas Hyde, Eoin MacNeill, George Russell, James
Connolly, and Countess Markievicz. On the other hand
he does ample justice to Yeats, Padraic Pearse, Jim
Larkin, Tom Clarke, and Father O'Hickey. A man of
fierce hatred and still fiercer love, O'Casey never treads
the middle path. Whether he is praising one or denouncing another, the focal point of interest is always
O'Casey.

The opinions expressed in this volume will vex many,
but there will be few who will fail to respond to the wild
hilarity that weaves its way through it, and to the superb
scenes of fantasy and farce. Take the scene in the
chapter "Prometheus Hibernica," where St Patrick,
rebuking a bishop for not controlling his flock at a Larkin
rally in 1913, gets into an argument with the figure of
Nelson perched on the pillar. St Patrick has the last say:

—Control yourselves, gentlemen, murmured the
stony voice of Nelson; try to control yourselves.
—Control yourself! shouted Patrick up at him. If
you could, you wouldn't send your murdherous polis
out to maim an' desthroy poor men lookin' for no more
than a decent livin'. Gah! If me crozier could only
reach up to you, I'd knock your other eye out![11]

Here, as Robert Heilman observes, one sees the fine concreteness even in O'Casey's fantasies where angels and Saints and statues chat and dispute, and where the dreams of lunatics take on a hard, factual presence.[12]

Inishfallen Fare Thee Well is the most impressive of the six volumes. O'Casey recalls with great clarity the years immediately following the Easter Rising, his grief at his mother's death and the pauper's funeral that accompanied it, the fight against the Black and Tans, and the heart-rending Civil War. Equally vivid is his account of the struggle to mount a play on the Abbey stage, and his meeting with Lady Gregory and W. B. Yeats. He writes about his success with great modesty: he gives the names and the plots of the plays the Abbey rejected, but dismisses *The Shadow of a Gunman* and *Juno and the Paycock* as his first and third play. He does not mention the rave notices these two plays received, but tells us that the first in its initial performance brought him less than £4, and the third £25. Nor does he mention *The Plough and the Stars* by name, and the title appears only in the adverse notices he quotes from jealous writers. The absence of names and dates (I doubt if there is a single date in the book) creates confusion for those not versed in the history of his plays; at times it is difficult to determine which play he is talking about. One reason for O'Casey's reticence may be that he never shared the public's enthusiasm for his Dublin plays.

O'Casey writes movingly of Yeats and most affectionately of Lady Gregory. This is as it should be, not only because they helped to launch him on the stage but also because he knew what the Abbey Theatre owed them. But he writes with vehemence against Æ (George Russell) in a chapter titled "Dublin's Glittering Guy." He attacks every aspect of Æ: the poet, the painter, the sage, and the economist, and dismisses him as a selfish, conceited, and arrogant man. Did O'Casey never hear of Æ's spirited defence of the workers during the 1913 lock-out, an event in which O'Casey himself played a part? Did he never read Æ's salutation to those who took part in the Easter Rising:

> Your dream had left me numb and cold
> But yet my spirit rose in pride,
> Re-fashioned in burnished gold
> The images of those who died;

and, did he never enjoy Æ's elfish sort of humour: the Æ who said on Monday, "Yeats has written a poem about a new Celtic god he has discovered called Orcill"; and, on Tuesday, "Yeats has torn up his poem. He has unfortunately discovered that his new Celtic god was really called Borcill"? Or the Æ who shook Yeats from one of his reveries with his "I am afraid, Willie, you are overlooking your father!" when the provident poet said that if he had his rights he would be Duke of Ormande? Still, all in all, the book lives up to Sean O'Faolain's estimation of it: "This is a book full of fine scorn and great courage; sound and fury; thirst for life; much love and more hate; and, in spite of everything that Dublin did to him, it is, above all, rich in loyalties to men and causes—and even to Dublin."[13]

Much of what O'Casey wrote in his next two volumes, *Rose and Crown* and *Sunset and Evening Star*, would be less enjoyable were it not for the old O'Casey traits: the gift of the gab, narrative detail, sharp observations, and incisive humour. A good part of the volumes is devoted to settling old scores, praising Yeats, Shaw, and the Soviet Union, denouncing the Catholic clergy and practices, and to expressing views on his own works and assailing all those who have dared to question the O'Casey word. From this stupendous effort, one thing emerges above all: the personality of the narrator himself. George Russell, who suffered most at O'Casey's hands, made the most significant comment. As early as

1928, when O'Casey was lambasting all those who disapproved of *The Silver Tassie*, he said:

Dear Sean,—You are creating a new character, and when you have finished annihilating your critics the portrait of the annihilator will be as vivid in the consciousness of your readers as Joxer or the Paycock.[14]

This has proved true. Deprived of a theatre, he took to writing autobiography and created a character worthy in every sense of the word to rank beside the immortals in literature.

REFERENCES

1. "O'Casey," *Kenyon Review*, 18, Autumn 1956, p. 664.
2. Robert Nye, "The Darlin' Man," *The Scotsman*, 7 Sept. 1963.
3. "A Great Dramatist's Approach to Autobiography," *The Commonweal*, 65, 25 Jan. 1957, pp. 441-2.
4. *I.K.D.*, p. 207.
5. See Cowasjee, p. xi.
6. *I.K.D.*, pp. 53-4.
7. *P.H.*, p. 232.
8. *D.U.W.*, p. 1.
9. *P.H.*, pp. 130-1.
10. P. Colum, "O'Casey: a Third Instalment," *Yale Review*, 36, Autumn 1946, p. 155.
11. *D.U.W.*, pp. 240-1.
12. "Definitions Needed," *Quarterly Review of Literature*, 4, no. 1, 1947, p. 109.
13. "O'Casey the Dubliner," *John o' London's Weekly*, 4 Feb. 1949, p. 71.
14. George Russell (Y.O.), "London with the Sun Out," in *The Irish Statesman*, 10, 4 Aug. 1928, p. 431.

BIBLIOGRAPHY

I. SEAN O'CASEY

The reader is referred for further bibliographical information to Saros Cowasjee, *Sean O'Casey: The Man Behind the Plays*, Edinburgh (Oliver & Boyd) 1963; New York (St Martin's Press) 1964; the list of Contents in *Feathers from the Green Crow*, ed. Robert Hogan, Columbia, Mo. (University of Missouri Press) 1962; London (Macmillan) 1963; and Ward Williamson's unpublished Ph.D. dissertation, *An Analytical History of American Criticism of the Works of Sean O'Casey* [1962], in the library of the State University of Iowa U.S.A. In Section 2 the dates in square brackets are of the first performance of the plays. Where editions subsequent to the first are used in *Collected Plays* they are listed in the Bibliography and marked*.

1. Collected Plays

Collected Plays, 4 vols., London (Macmillan) 1949-51, *1951-57. Vol. I (1949, *1957) contains *Juno and the Paycock, The Shadow of a Gunman, The Plough and the Stars, The End of the Beginning, A Pound on Demand*. Vol. II (1949, *1952) contains *The Silver Tassie, Within the Gates, The Star Turns Red*. Vol. III (1951) contains *Purple Dust, Red Roses for Me, Hall of Healing*. Vol. IV (1951) contains *Oak Leaves and Lavender, Cock-a-doodle Dandy, Bedtime Story, Time to Go*.

2. Plays

The Shadow of a Gunman [Dublin 1923]. In *Two Plays*, London (Macmillan) and New York (Macmillan) 1925.

Juno and the Paycock [Dublin 1924]. In *Two Plays*, London (Macmillan) and New York (Macmillan) 1925.

The Plough and the Stars [Dublin 1926]. London (Macmillan) and New York (Macmillan) 1926.

The Silver Tassie [London 1929]. London (Macmillan) and New York (Macmillan) 1928.

Within the Gates [London 1934]. London (Macmillan) 1933; New York (Macmillan) 1934.

The End of the Beginning [Dublin 1937]. A one-act play included in *Windfalls*, 1934.

The Star Turns Red [London 1940]. London (Macmillan) 1940.

Purple Dust [Boston 1944]. London (Macmillan) 1940.

Red Roses for Me [Dublin 1943]. London (Macmillan) 1942; New York (Macmillan) 1943.

Oak Leaves and Lavender [London 1947]. London (Macmillan) 1946;
    New York (Macmillan) 1947.
Cock-a-doodle Dandy [Newcastle-on-Tyne 1949]. London (Mac-
    millan) 1949.
Hall of Healing [New York 1952]. A one-act play in *C.P.*, III, 1951.
Bedtime Story [New York 1952]. A one-act play in *C.P.*, IV, 1951.
Time to Go [New York 1952]. A one-act play in *C.P.*, IV, 1951.
The Bishop's Bonfire [Dublin 1955]. London (Macmillan) and New
    York (Macmillan) 1955.
The Drums of Father Ned [Lafayette, Indiana 1959]. London (Mac-
    millan) and New York (St Martin's Press) 1960.
Behind the Green Curtains [Rochester, N.Y. 1962] London (Macmillan)
    and New York (St Martin's Press) 1961). This volume also in-
    cludes a play in two scenes, *Figuro in the Night* [New York 1962]
    and a one-act play, *The Moon Shines on Kylenamoe* [New York
    1962].
Kathleen Listens In [Dublin 1923]. A one-act play included in *F.G.C.*,
    1963.
Nannie's Night Out [Dublin 1924]. A one-act play included in *F.G.C.*,
    1963.

3. Autobiographies

I Knock at the Door, London (Macmillan) and New York (Macmillan)
    1939.
Pictures in the Hallway, London (Macmillan) and New York (Macmillan)
    1942.
Drums Under the Window, London (Macmillan) 1945; New York
    (Macmillan) 1946.
Inishfallen Fare Thee Well, London (Macmillan) and New York
    (Macmillan) 1949.
Rose and Crown, London (Macmillan) and New York (Macmillan)
    1952.
Sunset and Evening Star, London (Macmillan) and New York (Mac-
    millan) 1954.

4. Miscellaneous

Windfalls, London (Macmillan) and New York (Macmillan) 1934.
The Flying Wasp, London (Macmillan) 1937.
The Green Crow, New York (Braziller) 1956; London (W. H. Allen)
    1957.
Feathers from the Green Crow, Columbia (University of Missouri Press)
    1962; London (Macmillan) 1963.
Under a Colored Cap, London (Macmillan) and New York (St Martin's
    Press) 1963.

II. OTHERS

Only the more significant works referred to in the text are included here; also other works likely to be of use to students of O'Casey.

ARMSTRONG, WILLIAM A. "History, Autobiography, and *The Shadow of a Gunman*," in *Modern Drama*, 2, Feb. 1960.

——— (ed.). *Experimental Drama*, London 1963.

AYLING, RONALD. "Feathers Flying: Politics in the Early Life and Thought of Sean O'Casey," in *The Dubliner*, Spring 1964.

BOAS, GUY. "The Drama of Sean O'Casey," in *College English*, 10, Nov. 1948.

BROWN, IVOR. "Life by the Liffey," in *The Saturday Review*, 140, 21 Nov. 1925.

———. "Cautionary Tales," in *The Saturday Review*, 143, 18 Jun. 1927.

BRYNE, DAWSON. *The Story of Ireland's National Theatre*, Dublin 1929.

COLUM, PADRAIC. Review of *The Plough and the Stars*, in *Saturday Review of Literature*, 2, 12 Jun. 1926.

———. "Dublin Through the Abbey Theatre," in *The Road Round Ireland*, New York 1937.

———. "O'Casey: a Third Instalment," in *Yale Review*, 36, Autumn 1946.

"Correspondence: The Abbey Directors and Mr. O'Casey," in *The Irish Statesman*, 10, 9 June. 1928.

COSTON, HERBERT H. "Sean O'Casey: Prelude to Playwriting," in *The Tulane Drama Review*, 1, 1960.

COXHEAD, ELIZABETH. "Sean O'Casey," in *Lady Gregory*, London 1961.

DANIEL, WALTER C. "Patterns of Greek Comedy in O'Casey's *Purple Dust*," in *Bulletin of the New York Public Library*, 66, 1962.

E.S.A. "Mr. O'Casey Again," in *The Spectator*, 136, 29 May 1926.

ESSLINGER, PAT M. "Sean O'Casey and the Lockout of 1913: *Materia Poetica* of the Two Red Plays," in *Modern Drama*, 6, May 1963.

FALLON, GABRIEL. "The House on the North Circular Road: Fragment from a biography," in *Modern Drama*, 4, Dec. 1961. This is a special number devoted to O'Casey's life and works, and includes articles by W. A. Armstrong, Robert Hogan, Vincent C. De Baun, Katherine J. Worth, David Krause, and others.

———. "Profiles of a Poet," in *Modern Drama*, 7, Dec. 1964.

———. *Sean O'Casey: the Man I Knew*, London 1965.

FINDLATER, RICHARD. *The Unholy Trade*, London 1952.

GASSNER, JOHN. *Masters of the Drama*, 3rd rev. and enl. edn., New York 1954.

———. *Theatre in our Times*, New York 1954.

———. *Introduction to Selected Plays of Sean O'Casey*, New York 1954.

GREENE, DAVID H. "A Great Dramatist's Approach to Autobiography," in *The Commonweal*, 65, 25 Jan. 1957.

GREGORY, LADY AUGUSTA. *Journals (1916-30)*, ed. L. Robinson, London 1946.

GWYNN, STEPHEN. *Irish Literature and Drama*, London 1936.

HEILMAN, ROBERT. "Definitions Needed," in *Quarterly Review of Literature*, 4, No. 1, 1947.

HOGAN, ROBERT. *The Experiments of Sean O'Casey*, New York 1960.

HOWARD, MILTON. "Orwell or O'Casey?" in *Masses and Mainstream*, 8, Jan. 1955.

JOHNSTON, DENIS. "Sean O'Casey: an Appreciation," in *The Living Age*, 329, 17 Apr. 1926.

KAVANAGH, PETER. *The Story of the Abbey Theatre*, New York 1950.

KERR, WALTER. *How not to Write a Play*, New York 1955.

KNIGHT, GEORGE WILSON. *The Golden Labyrinth*, London 1962.

KOSLOW, JULES. *The Green and the Red*, New York 1949.

KRAUSE, DAVID. *Sean O'Casey, the Man and his Work*, London 1960.

———. "Sean O'Casey: 1880-1964," in *The Massachusetts Review*, 6, Winter-Spring 1965.

KRUTCH, JOSEPH WOOD. *"Modernism" in Modern Drama*, New York 1953.

LEWIS, ALLAN. "Irish Romantic Realism—Sean O'Casey," in *The Contemporary Theatre*, New York 1962.

DOROTHY MACARDLE. *The Irish Republic*, Dublin 1951.

MACCARTHY, DESMOND. "Juno and the Paycock," in *The New Statesman*, 26, 28 Nov. 1925.

———. *Drama*, London 1940.

MACLIAMMÓIR, MICHEÁL. "Problem Plays," in *The Irish Theatre*, ed. L. Robinson, London 1939. This volume includes a good study of O'Casey by Walter Starkie.

MACMURRAY, JOHN. *Creative Society*, London 1935.

MALONE, ANDREW E. *The Irish Drama*, New York 1929.

MERCIER, VIVIAN. *The Irish Comic Tradition*, Oxford 1962.

NATHAN, GEORGE JEAN. *Art of the Night*, New York 1928.

——— (ed.). *Five Great Modern Irish Plays*, New York 1941.

NICOLL, ALLARDYCE. *World Drama*, London 1949.

NYE, ROBERT. "The Darlin' Man," in *The Scotsman*, 7 Sep. 1963.

O'FAOLAIN, SEAN. *The Irish*, (Penguin) London 1947.

———. "O'Casey the Dubliner," in *John o' London's Weekly*, 4 Feb. 1949.

Ó MAOLÁIN, MÍCHEÁL. "An Ruathar Úd Agus A nDeachaigh Leis," in *Feasta*, May 1955.

O'SHAUGHNESSY, JOHN. "O'Casey: Forever Fare Thee Well," in *The Nation*, 184, 16 Mar. 1957.

POPKIN, HENRY. "O'Casey," in *Kenyon Review*, 18, Autumn 1956.

REES, LESLIE. "Remembrance of Things Past (II) On Meeting Sean O'Casey," in *Meanjin Quarterly*, 23, Dec. 1964.

RITCHIE, HARRY H. "The Influence of Melodrama on the Early Plays of Sean O'Casey," in *Modern Drama*, 5, Sept. 1962. The volume also contains a study of *Nannie's Night Out* by R. Ayling.

ROBINSON, LENNOX. *Towards an Appreciation of the Theatre*, Dublin 1945.

ROLLINS, RONALD G. "Sean O'Casey's Mental Pilgrimage," in *Arizona Quarterly*, 17, 1961.

RUDIN, SEYMOUR. "Playwright to Critic: Sean O'Casey's Letters to George Jean Nathan," in *The Massachusetts Review*, 5, Winter 1964.

Y.O. [GEORGE RUSSELL]. "London with the Sun Out," in *The Irish Statesman*, 10, 4 Aug. 1928.

SHAW, G. B. *John Bull's Other Island and Major Barbara*, London 1907.

SHIPP, H. "The Art of Sean O'Casey," in *The English Review*, 42, Jun. 1926.

SMITH, WINIFRED. "The Dying God in the Modern Theatre," in *Review of Religion*, 5, Mar. 1941.

TREWIN, J. C. *Dramatists of Today*, London 1953.

USSHER, ARLAND. *The Face and Mind of Ireland*, New York 1950.

WALDMAN, MILTON. "The Chronicles," in *The London Mercury*, 13, Feb. 1926.

WILLIAMS, RAYMOND. *Drama from Ibsen to Eliot*, London 1952.

WILLIAMSON, AUDREY. *Theatre of Two Decades*, London 1951.